PRAISE FOR

MW00781332

Dogged Optimism is an accomplished, inspiring piece of writing that had me completely hooked from the first page to the unexpected and gratifying end.

Gill Pavey, thebookreviewers.com

Dogged Optimism is a delightful read, as much about the ups and downs of owning a wilful dog as facing up to life, especially when it doesn't turn out as expected. Witty and warm, sometimes sad but never sentimental, it is a welcome addition to any bedside table.

Marianne Wheelaghan, *The Blue Suitcase* and the Scottish Detective Lady Mysteries

Anyone who's ever adored a dog can relate to this evocative, humorous tale of a woman and her beloved Australian terror – er, terrier – and their zany time together. Tissues optional, pet lovers required.

Molly Greene, The Gen Delacourt mysteries

Warm and genuine, this journey of a sassy Australian terrier and her spirited Aussie owner will charm you with its window into life Down

Under and inspire you with its insights into over-coming personal challenges.

Dawn Dicker, Writer & Content Strategist

A heart-warming tale of one woman's special bond with her four-legged friend. This book captures the eventful experiences a dog can bring into our life when we invite them into our home. A delightful read.

Tanya Arnold, Pupcake Queen

Dogged Optimism

Lessons in joy from a disaster-prone dog

BELINDA POLLARD

SMALL BLUE DOG
PUBLISHING

For Aunty Iris, who said,
"You really should write a book about that dog."

Author's note

MEMORY IS AN UNRELIABLE NARRATOR, AND OTHERS may remember these events differently. However, that would be their story to tell. This is my story, and this is what these events mean to me. I have changed many names and some details to respect the privacy of people who are not public figures. This is a story rather than a history, so I have sometimes combined, shortened or relocated events for the sake of the narrative. However, the core of the story is true to how the events and their impact live on in my life today.

This is of course *not* a book of instructions on how to raise a dog, medical advice for dogs, or anything of the kind. It's just one woman's story of living with a dog. If you want to know how to help your own dog, consult a vet or a dog behaviourist.

This book is written with Australian expressions and spelling, so if you're from another country prepare for some linguistic fun. Sure, you knew about color/colour, but what about organised, wilful and travelling? See if you can define the word "sook" by the time you've finished.

Acknowledgements

Thank you to the wise and gracious beta readers who critiqued my manuscript, and whose generous advice has made it a much better book. (Flaws that persist are mine, not theirs.) In alphabetical order they are:

- Dawn Dicker, content strategist and writer.
- Laura Zera, author of the upcoming *Wish I Had a River*.
- Lorraine Page, journalist and pre-published author.
- Molly Greene, author of the Gen Delacourt mysteries.
- Marianne Wheelaghan, author of *The Blue Suitcase* and the Scottish Detective Lady mysteries.
- Tanya Arnold, Pupcake Queen and author of the *Pupcakes* recipe book.

Thank you to my vet "Tom" and his assistant "Hayley", as well as his other staff, for going far beyond the call of duty in caring for my dogs and being my friends.

Thank you to my editor Jo Swinney who has been

much more than a wordsmith. She is a partner in the project – an encourager who sees the same vision, and brings it into clearer focus.

I honour my father Jim Pollard for teaching me how to love dogs, and my mother Barbara Pollard who believed I could write this book, and gently nagged me to get it done. Thank you, Mum, for helping in so many ways both practical and emotional – with the book project, with the dogs, and with life.

Finally, thanks to the One who made dogs wonderful and gave us the responsibility of caring for them kindly.

Contents

Author's note—vi

Acknowledgements—vii

It begins—1

Lesson 1:
Joy is not always a tidy thing—13

Lesson 2:
Joy is rarely where we expect to find it—31

Lesson 3:
Joy is having something to lose—45

Lesson 4:
Joy is worth fighting for—59

Lesson 5:
Joy is unpredictable—75

Lesson 6:
Joy is embracing your own uniqueness—93

Lesson 7:
Joy is having flexible expectations—105

Lesson 8:
Joy is making the best of life's imperfections—123

Lesson 9:
Joy can't get through if we're obsessed with misery—139

Lesson 10:
Joy is a new way of looking at things—153

Lesson 11:
Joy is bigger when life is harder—163

Lesson 12:
Joy survives in the worst of times—177

Lesson 13:
Joy is surrendering control—193

Lesson 14:
Joy isn't where most people think I should look—203

Lesson 15:
Joy is being yourself, not someone else—217

Lesson 16:
Be content, and joy might surprise you—237

Afterword—244

From the Author—246

Also by Belinda Pollard—248

It begins

THE DAYS THAT CHANGE OUR LIVES START MUCH THE same as other days. The sun rises, birds sing, tea brews. My life is not a movie, so no warning music plays as I scan the morning newspaper one sunny autumn Saturday in May 1998. In fact, the only soundtrack is the scraping of metal on crockery as I eat breakfast perched on a stool at the laminex-topped table in my parents' Brisbane kitchen – a thirty-something living at home with the folks again.

I'm surrounded by the familiar turquoise and white cupboards, and the floral cafe curtains that replaced the ones I accidentally set fire to while cooking chips. It's as though I've time-travelled to my early twenties. That's when the three of us last ate at this table every day, after the last of my four older brothers and sisters married. Their families are growing. Meanwhile, a lot of people seem to assume I've chosen the single life. What else can I tell them? "I was working so hard I forgot to get married." "I'm useless at relationships." Let them assume what they want, and I'll talk about the lone-liness to my close friends in private.

An entry in the pet classifieds catches my eye and I pause, cereal spoon halfway to mouth, milk dripping:

Aust Terrier pups vacc blue/tan v. healthy
From $250.

I can decipher the code because I'm on a mission – I've been reading these unpunctuated unsentenc-es for months. The ad tells me that these pups are the colour of the Australian terriers we had when I was a kid. They're vaccinated, so the breeders are responsible people.

A plan formulates in my mind. My mother, she of the stainless steel immune system, is emerging from one of her rare-but-monumental doses of the flu, and she's well enough to have cabin fever. An outing?

"Pet store, can I help you?" says a voice at the other end of the phone line. I expected a private home. In my youth, our puppies came from relatives and friends. I'm nervous about a pet shop. I've seen puppies sitting in their own waste, and heard about them being left to cry alone overnight. I can't view the animal's parents or meet the people who bred them. Choosing a puppy is a delicate process, requiring patience and careful selection. Some of my friends' marriages haven't lasted as long as a dog.

I clear my throat and regroup. "Did you post an ad for Australian terrier puppies?"

"Yes, that's us."

"Are they the old-fashioned kind? The working dog with coarse hair? Or are they Australian silkies?" All the descriptions I've read before this one have been inaccurate.

"No, they're genuine Australian terriers."

Heck, it's just an outing, Belinda. "Well, we might come and look at them this morning."

I say to Mum, "What do you think? It's not as if I'm going to buy a puppy today. But you can cuddle one, I'll buy you some coffee and cake, and then you can come back home for a nap."

She smiles. A glance passes between her and Dad.

❧

FIVE TINY, SHORT-HAIRED BLACK-AND-TAN PUPPIES ROMP among clean shredded newspaper. Each has a black face and brown eyebrows. They remind me of a Doberman's mini-me. The ones I knew from childhood had docked tails. I now think that sounds like an awful thing to do to a pup, and yet I'm flummoxed by this forest of five long skinny tails pointing skyward. They look like spears of black asparagus falling to left then right, or sticking straight up as the wearer leaps into a growly puppy-attack on a sibling.

I'm shown a copy of the mother's pedigree. A photo of the father is on display, but not his pedigree. Clearly, this union took place on the wrong side of the kennel blanket.

The salesgirl confesses with a smile, "We take them home with us at night. I'm going to miss them when they're all gone."

I might as well take a good look at them. I prefer a female because we always had female dogs when I was growing up.

There are only two females left. One is fat and fluffy. Placed on the industrial carpet, she waddles over to a colourful display of aquarium fish accessories, collapses onto her well-rounded bottom and starts gnawing on the shelf. Hmm. That looks like a bad hobby.

Contestant Number Two is thin and small, the runt of the litter, not as pretty. She hits the carpet running and disappears into the dim recesses of the pet shop. I follow and watch as she peers behind counters and down aisles, fearless, an explorer. I feel a tug somewhere in my chest. But I'm not getting a puppy today.

We share cuddles all round. The fat and timid puppy snuggles into Mum's chest and she smiles. The thin puppy wriggles and squirms, anxious to be off and doing.

I tell the salesgirl, "We'll go and have a coffee and think about it." It will be easier to just walk away once I'm out of the store.

At the cafe, I spoon chocolate mud cake into my mouth. It's thick and heavy and it's a struggle to talk around it, but I manage. "I wasn't going to buy a dog today… but what do you think?"

"It's your decision," Dad says, looking intently at the froth he's scooping off his cappuccino.

My parents have always been careful to stand back while their children are making big decisions, but I'm hoping they'll break the habit today. No luck, although I can tell by their surreptitious sideways looks at each other that they are wary of an impulsive choice.

"I've been looking for a pup for a while. It's so hard to find genuine Australian terriers. What if I can't find another one? And at least these ones seem to have been well-cared-for…" A poor decision could dog me – excuse the lousy pun – for the next fifteen years. And since I'm living with my parents at the moment, it's their problem too. I suspect Mum favours the fat, fluffy pup, although she's being discreet about it.

"I like the adventurous one," I say, "but what if she turns out to be a nightmare?"

やく

AN HOUR LATER WE ARE DRIVING HOME WITH DAD AT the wheel of my car because there's two in the back seat: one terrified woman, and one bold puppy.

I am now a dog owner. They don't give refunds.

Will she get carsick? If she does, will I get any on me? I hold the little bundle up at shoulder height so she can see out the window, hoping that will fend off stomach upheaval. She seems barely aware of my presence. At least her fascination with the world flying by outside has stopped her wriggling.

What on earth am I going to call her?

At home, I'm confronted by the temporarily forgotten reality of Mackie, my parent's insecure kelpie-Labrador mix, a rescue pet with a history we can only guess at. He's had nothing but love since joining the Pollard family, but the echoes of past wrongs sometimes govern his behaviour in strange ways. What if he attacks Nameless?

I place her on the concrete patio and stand back to watch, tense and ready to intervene. Mackie sniffs the pup in open suspicion, ears flattened, legs stiff. As we mill around, two black dogs and three humans with fourteen legs between us, his jealousy mounts. Thankfully he doesn't bite but reverts to his kelpie blood, herding the interloper away from his humans.

Although the other dog towers over her – at least four times her height and ten times heavier – Nameless doesn't cringe. She sits back on her heels, gives just one peremptory displeased yap… and walks right through underneath him to her waiting public on the other side.

෴

Nameless is the fourth Australian terrier in my life.

When I was a kid, we got our dogs from people we knew. Back in that simpler time none of us had heard of the horror of puppy farms, and only rich people could afford to go to the pedigree breeders. A family with a good dog put it together with someone else's good dog of the same breed, and the progeny were shared around to loving homes.

We had a series of ginger cats too, but ours were

usually rangy farm cats given away for free. Their general approach to anything human was a look that said "Drop dead", and a stalking off to see if they could catch a mouse somewhere. I tried to stroke them enough times to know what a cat scratch feels like, but I didn't bond to them the way I bonded to the dogs.

When I was small there was Min, often cranky and prone to the occasional warning nip. Who could blame her, with five kids poking and prodding?

Buttons loved to chase cane toads, an introduced pest whose neck sacs brim with deadly neurotoxin. Usually we got them off her quickly enough – except for one time. I have a vivid memory of gripping her, trying to hold her still on the floor of the car as it cornered fast and my shoulder crashed painfully into the door, my eyes just inches from her glazed ones, her body bent back on itself in toxic spasm. There was no antidote but the vet sedated her to give her body a chance to deal with the poison, and we waited, and she recovered. Surprisingly, Buttons made it to old age. She went almost completely blind, which mercifully put an end to the toad chasing. Her hearing went too, but she could still hear the rattle of the dinner dish, and the whining of Dad's power saw as she lay snoozing in the sun, sleep-howling in response to the call of the wild.

But the one who really created a dog-shaped compartment in my heart was Jellybean – a smart dog, full of mischievous doggy smiles. Though less than knee-high, she was athletic and could easily leap our fence when she felt so inclined. Then we'd have cause to reconsider the wisdom of our naming choice as we walked through suburban streets calling "Je-e-elly-be-e-an!" In the photos I took of her with my first SLR film camera, she looks drunk or deranged, but it's actually just her dreamy "tummy-rub face" – the only way I could get her to sit still long enough. She was my friend when it seemed the whole world was against me. I probably spent roughly half of puberty slumped on the back steps, blubbing because girls had been mean to me at school or the cat had eaten another one of my guinea pigs. The slurp of a warm tongue along my dangling hand would be the signal to look into melting brown eyes and be comforted.

I have travelled the world and lived in various Australian cities, always in rental accommodation with landlords who had a no-pet policy. I have patted other people's dogs and yearned for one of my own, another Jellybean to love me no matter what.

At last my life is shifting into a new era. A few months ago I took the plunge, resigning from a good job with a Sydney publisher and a contract that still had two years to run. For years I have dreamed of starting a freelance writing and editing business. I have my former employer's blessing plus the guarantee they'll send me freelance work. My parents have offered me a place to live while I get started – I'll pay board, but it's a lot less than rent. They've even been incredibly sensitive about it, helping me avoid the ignominy of sleeping on Holly Hobby bed sheets beneath cutesy pictures on the childhood-bedroom wall. Instead, under the house, they've displaced a lot of their own belongings to create a small flat. I've got a narrow bedroom, a sitting room lined with bookshelves my Dad built decades ago into the wall where my homework desk used to stand, a sunny "home office" corner, and off to the side of my mother's laundry, a mostly-mine bathroom. Outside the back door is a toilet that's for use by anyone working in the yard, but in practice that one is mostly-mine too.

Beyond the patio and the classic Australian rotary clothesline is a big yard. A well-fenced, dog-friendly yard. My parents love dogs. I have always been around dogs so it will be as easy as falling off a log to incorporate one into my life. After all these years of waiting, finally it is time.

THE SQUISHY BALL THAT WILL DIE A THOUSAND DEATHS.

LESSON 1:

Joy is not always a tidy thing

I SURFACE THROUGH MULTIPLE DENSE LAYERS OF SLEEP and blankets. Someone is singing Chinese opera, loudly. I peer at the clock radio: 4:03 am. At least four hours till my weekend rising time.

The thought coagulates in my head: "Nameless is yelping." Her cries amplify off the brick walls of the outdoor toilet. It makes a splendid echo chamber.

My parents are Outdoor Dog people and there's no changing that, but I couldn't bear to put Nameless alone in her shiny new kennel on her first night. After a period of chaos trying to settle her upstairs on the back veranda – an indoor-outdoor compromise – I had finally got her asleep on a blanket on the turquoise vinyl floor tiles of my loo, just outside the back door.

The cacophony continues. She's going to wake the neighbours. Someone really should do something about it.

4.04 am: Oh. That someone would probably be me.

4.06 am: It must be the change of food. She's had diarrhoea, several times. And sat in it. And walked around and sat in it again. The toilet floor resembles a most unsavoury Jackson Pollock painting. The puppy's hair is matted with runny poo. I stand and stare, barefoot and fuddle-headed in my pyjamas.

There's nothing else for it: Nameless must have a bath. Right now, in the cold dark night.

And there's no one else to do it. Despite being a loving aunty to a dozen children, for the past fifteen years I have cuddled and cooed at baby after baby, while cleverly evading every single nappy change and vomit clean-up. It has even become a subject of wry pride and cheeky determination. There was one near miss when a babysitting friend didn't know how to operate a disposable nappy. I pulled the tabs for her as I'd seen done so many times before, but she was still the one holding the child and my record remained intact – just.

But now I'm going to have to deal with something much worse. I'm not sure they make rubber gloves thick enough for this.

As warm water thunders into the stainless steel laundry tub, I gaze through my own tired reflection in the glass louvres to the inky black silence outside. Normally I'm nervous in my parents' huge yard at night, but right now I don't care how many prowlers might be staring in at me from among the clustered trees.

I pick up the puppy as though she's a bomb, wishing my arms were twice as long. I bathe her gently and rinse her carefully. I dry her thoroughly with a towel and put her in my bathroom. I shut the door so she can't escape, and venture out to deal with her floor painting. She starts yelping again, but she'll have to wait.

I clean the toilet floor as well as I can with thick rubber gloves, a cloth and a bucket of disinfectant, being extremely careful not to stand in anything. I'll mop it thoroughly in the morning when there's more light and I've had more sleep.

I return to the bathroom to retrieve the puppy.

She's had diarrhoea.

And sat in it.

Again.

I stare, flummoxed.

The whole world is asleep. Everyone who doesn't have a new puppy, that is. *And possibly one or two people with real problems*, I think, but then bat the worthy thought aside. I've heard not a single creak of the floorboards upstairs. My parents are either managing to sleep right through this debacle, or they are choosing to pretend that's what they're doing.

I return to the laundry tub and run warm water. I bathe her gently. Again. I dry her thoroughly. Again.

I return her to the outdoor loo, and tuck her up as warmly as I can in her bedding. Surely her bowel must be empty by now.

After I shut the door on her she creates a ruckus, but by the time I've got the bathroom floor clean(ish), all is silent. I creep off to bed, exhausted and hopeful.

In the morning, Mum comes downstairs to find me furtively slopping hot disinfectant around. I've risen at a disgusting hour to do it so she wouldn't have to know the full horror of what has transpired on her floors. My mother's housekeeping standards would shame most hospitals.

"You're up early," she says. "What are you doing?"

I pause a moment and lean on the mop. "Um, we had a bit of an incident in the night. She had diarrhoea." I look out from under my eyebrows at Mum, tentative, wondering what reaction I'm going to get. Nameless lollops happily nearby on the sunny grass, giving Mackie a razz as he slinks around, affronted and confused. From her appearance, no one would suspect this puppy had ever felt unwell.

"Oh," Mum says. That's all. No pressing for further details, no inspection of my cleaning efforts. She must be off her game; perhaps it's just a hangover from the flu. But I'm almost sure I see a small smile on her face as she walks away.

৩

As night draws in on my second day of being a dog owner and I'm dithering about how to manage it, Dad says, "Why don't you just put her in her kennel?"

I'm not sure about this, but then how can it be any worse than what happened in the outdoor toilet? It's a sturdy little white-painted timber kennel that my father built for me a year earlier in a moment of fleeting optimism when my Sydney landlady considered allowing a dog. Before Dad retired, he was a civil engineer who spent his days managing important road, drainage and water supply projects, but working wood with his hands makes him happy. He even designed the kennel as a flat-pack construction so that it was easy to transport. Just undo the wing nuts, fold the walls and floor inside the roof, and slip it into the back of the car. The kennel has been lying flat in my parents' shed since I returned from Sydney, waiting for just such a time as this.

Dad wants to put it next to Mackie's kennel, a subdivision of doghouses under the guava tree, but I object. "She needs to be close to the house. She'll be scared. And there might be toads."

"Oh, we don't get toads in that spot. And there's not many now anyway." We're heading into winter, and they do go into hibernation in the cooler months.

"It only takes one."

As we learned the hard way with Buttons in my teens, cane toads can be the blight of a Brisbane terrier owner's life. Introduced to North Queensland from South America by some genius back in the 1930s in an attempt to control the sugar cane beetle, they quickly spread south, killing a lot of native wildlife and none of the cane beetles. Ugly, warty creatures with grey-brown, leathery skin, they have poison glands behind their eyes that squirt when pressed – for example, by the teeth of a dog. They are the sumo wrestlers of the amphibious world. The biggest specimens can weigh as much as 2.5 kg (5.5 lbs) and be nearly as long as a person's forearm, but thankfully I've never seen one quite *that* big. Hot summer nights might see as many as thirty of them scattered across our lawn catching insects, and their trill, like someone hammering on a hollow log, joins all the other raucous night-sounds of the Australian bush.

Hoover, my brother's Australian terrier (named for his eating technique rather than an American president) died in the process of killing a cane toad. Mackie, a herding breed, has never shown an interest in things that crawl or hop, so he's safe. But Nameless is a terrier. This early in the relationship, I have no idea where her instincts will lead her.

My negotiation with Dad ends with the kennel placed on the gravel pathway alongside the house, close to the back door. Toads don't come right up to the house.

As the darkness comes down on Night Two, I nervously leash the puppy to a hook outside the kennel door so she'll know where she's meant to be. Will she be okay? She considers her options, and hops inside.

The night passes quietly and calmly. In the morning she's relaxed and happy to see me. Apparently, Nameless feels right at home in a kennel.

❧

FOR TWO DAYS, I AGONISE OVER WHAT TO CALL THE PUP-py. Name after name is considered, discussed with my parents, and rejected. Amused by the long titles on her half-a-pedigree and the way they hark back to the previous generations of dogs, I decide to give her an equally long name inspired by my grandparents. Dad's parents owned a farm west of Sydney called Karinya, meaning something like "happy home" in one of the Aboriginal languages. Mum's mother lived at Killarney Vale on the New South Wales coast. Both places hold special memories for me.

And so Killarney Karinya joins the family.

Puppies are cute so we want to hold them. Puppies are young, so they'd rather play and explore. But I work out that if I wait till naptime there will be an opportunity. A cuddle where one party is unconscious is perhaps not quite as meaningful as it would be if she'd climbed into my lap voluntarily, but I'm a new dog mother and I'll take what I can get. I lean on the back fence chatting with a neighbour, a small pup lying along my forearm fast asleep.

I take her to the vet for a "new puppy" check-up. Choosing her medical overseer is thankfully more straightforward than choosing her name. Tom the vet is a big, tall Aussie with a laconic, straight-faced sense of humour. His rooms are simple and he has no truck with pet feng shui and other fripperies of the modern consumer world. However, over the years I've watched him rescue several Pollard dogs from the brink of death, and that's all the recommendation I need.

He examines Killarney and listens to her heart. "Yep, she's good," he declares.

I haven't met the nurse before. Hayley turns out to be a serious young woman with kind eyes and a gentle voice. She sends me home with worming medicines and a timetable for Killarney's series of vaccinations.

I'm doing everything by the book. This dog will be healthy. She will be perfect.

જી

FURIOUS YAPPING STARTLES ME FROM MY WORK. IT'S OUR fifth night, and Killarney has dined and been put to bed, leashed happily to her kennel. I race outside to rescue her from unknown dangers, and stand stock still for half a second trying not to laugh.

A huge cane toad is sitting on the path facing Killarney. It is nearly as big as her, and stolid in the face of her fearsome warning. Toads have a great poker face.

She is trying so hard to back away from it that she has actually dragged the kennel a few inches down the path with her – a feat akin to me dragging a king-sized bed with one hand.

I disentangle her and pick her up for a soothing embrace while herding the toad away with my feet. She recovers quickly from the shock. "Well hopefully that means you're going to be toad-proof, little pup."

But the thought lingers and takes root in my mind.

"Dad, can't she stay on the veranda till she's a bit older?"

"She'll be all right. Toads don't usually come near the house."

"That one did."

The veranda is ruled out. Neither of my parents wants a long-term hairy resident in their favourite spot. After a lot of debate, we settle on an eccentric solution from the Pollard school of lateral thinking.

The core feature is a large metal trailer Dad uses to cart rubbish to the dump, move furniture from place to place, and so on. Its sides are solid metal for a short distance, and then above that a heavy wire grid. He cobbles together a roof for the trailer from his selection of old timbers and tarps, and places her kennel inside.

With a bit of argument and pulling of heartstrings, I negotiate to get it moved nearer the house. After all, she's tiny. She can't be way up the back yard.

That night, Killarney hops into her kennel for bed again, but this time it's in the trailer, held aloft far above the hopping of toads. She is the queen of her castle, and she takes it all in her stride.

❧

WE SETTLE INTO A ROUTINE. MACKIE HAS ACCEPTED THE interloper in his domain, because what else can he do? Killarney sleeps soundly at night. I'm getting on with life as a shiny new pet owner. Sure, the first few weeks were rough at times, but thankfully all is clear sailing from now on.

I had several journeys already planned when Killarney came to live with me, and thanks to the convenience of built-in petsitters I can go on them without fear or inconvenience.

I jet off to Sydney to help a friend celebrate her fortieth birthday in a creaking historic mansion in the misty southern highlands. I visit friends in Coffs Harbour who live near the beach. I fly a 13,000 kilometre round trip to the remote Pilbara region of northern Western Australia, as part of a group helping a local church to support their community.

Amid the vast emptiness of the outback, there is a clutch of small towns together, formed around the booming mining industry and traditional aboriginal settlements. While my parents are playing with my puppy, I'm being greeted by the huge, protective dogs everyone seems to own in the remote northwest. Arriving at one home for dinner, I'm on alert when I'm met at the front door by an enormous Rottweiler – until I notice the fluffy toy in her mouth, the "aw shucks" ear position, and the little waggle in her stumpy tail. While my parents are getting up early in the cold to let Killarney out of her castle, I'm gazing at a huge, brassy sky above rows of tussock-covered hillocks. To me, they look like stegosaurs asleep in the sun. Yes, it's winter, but it's hot enough to need air-conditioning in the daytime. I'm glad we didn't come in summer, when the temps climb into the 40s Celsius (104F+) and can stay that high right through the night.

Anything could be going on at home, but Killarney is in good hands. Pet ownership is a lark.

On my return, I decide to start taking Killarney for walks. Everyone says dogs are good for exercise, and I certainly need some, even if she doesn't. Now that I'm working at home, it's surprising how much incidental exercise I'm missing out on. I've rejoined my mother's physical culture club so I dance to music once a week, but I mostly forget to practice between classes.

Although Killarney is tied up at night, she's never walked on a leash. I give her a trial run in the backyard. I clip it to her collar and start walking.

Killarney prefers to go in another direction. The collar bites her neck and she is displeased. She is growing bolder by the day – and she was pretty bold to start with. She wrestles with the leash, whips her head from side to side and frowns fiercely.

She's not the only determined one, and I'm bigger.

We set out for our first excursion around the block on a sunny morning after rain. Her opening gambit is to thrash about protesting the leash, but once we step beyond her known universe all that is forgotten. She strains forward – almost strangling herself in her eagerness to see what's next. She has worlds to discover and conquer.

We pass a woman walking an obedient spaniel. I smile and nod. "Good morning." Killarney greets them too, eyes bright, tongue lolling, breath rasping as she drags me along.

It's a big block, about two kilometres ($1^1/4$ mile). Was it this long when I was a kid? Halfway in, I realise we may have bitten off more than a small puppy should be chewing on her tiny legs – not to mention an unfit woman. But Killarney shows no signs of slowing down, still pulling at the full reach of her leash.

Some people haven't mown their grass in a while. In places she is just ears and a tail moving through the grass.

On the last uphill stretch it really is getting a bit much for her, though she'd continue if she could. I bend down to pick her up, my hand under her chest, pressing her back against my shoulder. She is still small and light enough to hold in one hand. As I puff my way home, she surveys the world with bright eyes, ready for anything.

ℰᴈ

KILLARNEY IS GROWING INTO HER ADULT APPEARANCE. Her hair is lengthening and becoming more feathery. Her colouring is softening – still dark, but heading towards the silvery grey they call "blue". Her brown eyebrows have spread and merged, covering her whole head in tan. She might soon be blonde, like Jellybean all those years ago.

I've tried her on various balls, but she doesn't play fetch like Mackie does. She plays catch and kill. Her favourite is a bright and squishy plastic ball, bigger than her head. When I kick it, she leaps on it and sinks razor sharp puppy teeth into it, growling ferociously and giving it a death shake. When she's sure it has learned its lesson, she flings it back near my feet, eyes bright, waiting for it to fly again. That ball dies a thousand deaths a day.

Growing up around Mackie seems to have affected her strangely. She has taken to weeing like a male dog, cocking her leg. She often changes her mind about which leg it will be, so that it turns into a kind of hovering handstand with first one hind leg and then the other going skyward.

She and Mackie are learning to get along. It's an uneasy truce – mostly in the sense that when she's truculent, he's uneasy. They play together each day. One day I find them lying together, her small body curled into the curve formed by his legs and belly. They are friends, even if his role sometimes has a little of the hostage about it.

Mackie is Dad's dog. Unlike me, my father has never been overly tactile with our pets. They get an occasional pat on the head, or a word or two of conversation. Mackie is Dad's shadow, his apprentice as he toils in his big steel shed, building and fixing things.

While he works, Mackie hovers among the relics of

Pollard history. The big green canvas marquee-style tent that held seven camp stretchers in a row for all those beachside holidays at Maroochydore, back when fish and chips was the only takeaway in town. The beautifully-painted stage scenery that Dad built for Mum's physical culture concerts over several decades – concerts that always ran exactly to schedule, and in which I danced alongside other girls dressed as lollipops or "naturellement, the Aristocats". The ship-shape red and cream sailing dinghy, a Dad-project that in my unreliably-stretchy child's memory filled our garage with the scent of wood shavings for years on end, and still carries in its timbers the echoes of many a noisy race out on Moreton Bay.

Now, Dad has two apprentices. As he walks to the shed he has an entourage. "Hello, small dog. Hello medium-sized dog."

A good friend from Sydney phones for a chat, and she's a dog lover so I tell her amusing stories about my new puppy.

"Oh, you've got a dog now?" she says. "I guess that means you'll be staying in Brisbane permanently." She sounds a little crestfallen. It's nice of her to miss me, but I don't know what she means.

"Why would that stop me moving if I wanted to?" Some people have the strangest ideas.

HAVE TRAILER, PROBABLY WON'T TRAVEL.

LESSON 2:
Joy is rarely where we expect to find it

WINTER MOVES INTO SPRING, AND MY NEW BUSINESS is floundering. The publisher I used to work for in Sydney is still sending me books to edit, but the money doesn't seem to add up to much. When we were planning before I left Sydney, the hourly rate the union recommended seemed too high so we'd negotiated something lower. I'm beginning to think the union knows more about the expenses of this gig than I do. But I don't know how to raise my rates. Asking for money terrifies me.

As for freelance journalism, I've worked like mad to get my articles accepted. I chase newspapers and magazines around the country. I try the techniques I learned at a freelance journalism conference: use one set of research to create multiple unique articles for different publishers. I'd been imagining a world where I could make a modest living with part of the week and have time left over to write the novel that has been burning a hole in my brain for three years.

But the union-card freelance rates that inspired such hopes back in the safety of a full-time job in Sydney are apparently a fantasy.

One newspaper offers me $80 for an article that took days to write. I accept the offer because, heck, it's $80 I didn't have before.

Dog food is yet another expense, but at least I've still got a roof over my head.

"Put a hold on your board payments," says Dad.

"You can pay us back when your finances improve," says Mum.

I'd been secretly hoping they'd say, "Don't worry about paying board at all until you're rich and famous." But then, I'm actually glad they made me work for things all my life. I got ten cents pocket money when I was a small child, but I could earn more if I watered the plants or dug prickles out of the lawn. I discovered early that a pleasure you've worked for is sweeter than one you've been handed on a plate. Even now, although I joke about marrying a millionaire I don't want to be too rich because where's the motivation in that? Enough to pay the bills each month without having to think about it, and something still to strive for. That's wealth, to me.

A few months ago, I applied for a casual job with

a market research company to supplement my income. I was remembering stories I'd heard back at university in the eighties about how market research paid well, if you could get the work. Well, things have obviously gone downhill. Market research nineties-style apparently involves a group job interview where almost everyone who can stand up and speak English is offered a position with a starting rate of the Australian minimum wage. Back in April, I said to myself, "I'm not that desperate." And I walked out of there.

But after a few more months of stretching the ends ever more tightly to try to make them meet, I've realised that lousy money is better than no money. When I see another market research job advertised, I apply. This time when they offer me and a bunch of others the job at minimum wage, I sign up to do their two-day training. My mission, should I choose to accept it, is to do a survey to find out people's reactions to a particular series of television advertisements. I have to walk up to complete strangers in a public place when they are relaxing on the weekend. I can set my own start and finish hours within reason, as I will be paid for hours worked. If I don't achieve my full set of interviews on Saturday, I can go back on Sunday to complete them. But by the end of the weekend I must have fourteen surveys to submit.

The thought terrifies me.

But I need the money.

I nervously prepare for my first day out on my own. No supervisor or colleague; just me. My new boss recommends the Botanic Gardens along the Brisbane River. All day Friday, I gaze out my window as rain pours down.

Can I get out of doing it, if the weather is bad?

But I need the money.

Saturday dawns bright and clear, and I breathe a sigh of relief, sort of. I choose a spring outfit of pastel top and cream pants with a nice, crisp crease down the front. The shoes need to be flat since I'll be walking around a park in them all day, but nevertheless they are smart, and also cream. It makes a change from the track pants and slippers I normally wear to work at home.

I go outside to let Killarney out of her castle and serve breakfast. Some affection from her might help calm my stomach, which is roiling with nerves.

Her abode has now been moved up the back under the mango tree, Dad's patience for a trailer outside the back door having been exhausted. I pick my way carefully across the wet grass. Killarney is up and dancing. I pull the bolt that allows the back of the trailer to drop down. It lands with a brown splash that I neatly evade. She leaps down after it, does a quick Macarena in the mud, full of the joy of morning, and then launches herself at my legs. My crisp-creased cream-clad legs.

You may be thinking that any woman who would combine mud, a puppy and light-coloured clothing probably has a few kangaroos loose in the top paddock. But my brain is in my other handbag today unfortunately, and all I can do is stare at brown paw prints all down my pants and yell: "You stupid dog!"

Killarney tries to appease me by jumping up on my crisp-creased cream-clad legs again.

At seven on a Saturday, I'm sure my neighbours enjoy the scream that follows.

⌘

I TRY TO CALM MYSELF BY TAKING DEEP BREATHS WHILE I stand at the laundry sink. Come what may, I'm wearing these pants. I remove as much moisture as I can by folding the pants between towels, rolling them up tight and squeezing – one of the laundry tips of the veteran traveller. Should I iron them dry? No, it's not a good fabric for that. I shrug and put them back on, still damp. The car I bought for driving in Sydney's cooler climate has no air-conditioning; it's an hour's drive to the Botanic Gardens; it's a hot day.

As I walk into the gardens, my clothes are nearly dry but my palms are damp. Usually I love this green oasis a few blocks downhill from the central business district, sloping down to the wide, brown, sleepy Brisbane River in a place where it does a hairpin bend. The lush lawns and gracious spreading trees always make me feel like I'm back in the colonial era. There's even a native macadamia tree planted in 1858 that still produces nuts.

Today I wish I *was* in the colonial era, because they probably didn't do market research then.

I hold my clipboard up in full view, swallow the lump in my throat and approach a young woman who is watching her children play.

"Excuse me. Sorry to bother you. Would you be interested in doing a survey?"

She looks at me like I've escaped from an asylum. "No thanks."

The next one holds up her hand and says, "I don't want to buy whatever you're selling."

"I'm not selling anything." I point to my nametag, the proof of all veracity.

"Yeah, sure you're not."

I want to stand and fight about it – if there's anything I hate, it's being called a liar to my face – but it would be unprofessional. Besides, she's walked off.

Finally, a man takes pity on me. Perhaps he too has had to do a horrible job sometime in his life. But the initial screening questionnaire excludes him – he works in marketing. Thwarted, I want to cry, but instead I thank him most sincerely and wish him a good day.

At the end of a day of anxious stalking, I have ten hard-won surveys in the bag. Only ten. I will have to go back tomorrow and do the other four. I am thirty-four years old with two university degrees, doing a job I find terrifying for minimum wage.

At home, I want to sit on the back steps and sob, but there'll be no consoling licks or sympathetic eyes from Killarney. Whenever she sees me crying, she doesn't know what it is and trots off to do something more interesting until I've finished. She knows what her big squishy plastic ball is though, and so I kick it around for her and she leaps on it, growling, gives it a death shake, throws it back at me and barks and waggles. I kick it for her again and you know what? That's not bad therapy either.

I'M WALKING DOWN TO THE SHED AND KILLARNEY IS romping in the grass with Mackie when my ears are split by a high-pitched doggy scream. Killarney runs helter-skelter round the yard, yelping in agony and fear, and stopping occasionally to bite at her foot.

My first thought is *green ant.* They are big, glossy, black ants with a green sheen, the bane of a Brisbane backyard, especially for a young child who gets tired during play and decides to flop down on the grass right onto a hidden nest. They have a sting like a wasp. And they have a tendency to latch on and refuse to let go.

I chase Killarney as she runs, and scoop her up in my arms, fighting to see between her toes as she wriggles and yelps. Sure enough, it's a green ant.

A fierce and primal emotion surges up through my body as she whimpers. I battle to remove the ant, careless of whether it might bite me too. I run with her in my arms to her water bowl and plunge her foot into the cold water. Cold will ease the pain; I'm not even sure how I know that.

For years I've listened to single friends mope about how much they want a baby. I've made sympathetic noises while secretly thinking, "Yes, they're gorgeous to cuddle… but so much work!" I've always thought I must have been standing behind the door when maternal instincts were distributed.

I hold Killarney there with her foot in the water for several minutes, and make soothing, clucking noises as she gradually calms down. My eyes widen. Who am I becoming?

✂

IN THE CORNER OF THE BACK YARD BESIDE THE MANGO tree lurks the black bean, a majestic rainforest tree with large, heavy seedpods. They crack open to release up to five glossy dark brown seeds, each the size of a flattened golf ball.

And Killarney is chewing one.

I grab it from her and she looks disappointed, waiting for me to give it back. The dark coating of the seed is missing in several places and there are chips out of the creamy interior, which are now presumably inside her. I stare from puppy to saliva-coated seed in horror. What if it's poisonous?

I dial Poisons Information, trying to think of ways to disguise the fact that I'm calling about a puppy rather than a child. "Do you know if seeds from the black bean tree are poisonous?"

A pleasant and efficient woman replies, "Just a

moment. I'll look it up." Pause. "It says they can cause stomach upset. If you're concerned, see your doctor."

I call the vet, but he's not too worried. "Just watch her. Let us know."

I watch Killarney like a hawk for hours as she romps, her usual puppy self. We've dodged a bullet, apparently.

A few weeks later, I walk out the back door and Killarney is lying on her belly on the grass, chewing enthusiastically. The bedraggled remnants of a different kind of seed, thick as a man's thumb and four times longer, are gripped between her front paws. She looks up and waggles her tail, then resumes her meal.

I grab the seedpod from her, but as much as half of it is missing, presumably eaten.

"Dad!"

"What?"

"What's this?" I wave the mangled thing at him as he sticks his head out of the shed.

"I don't know." He frowns, peering. "Looks like a seedpod from the golden rain tree."

"Killarney was eating it."

"Probably won't do her any harm."

"How would *you* know?" My voice rises indignantly on the "you". I'm thinking not only of the potential danger, but the awkwardness of having to phone Poisons Information again.

There are no golden rain trees in the yard. "Did you take her out the front with you this morning?"

"Yes, I took them both when I went to the letter-box." *Because I'm so kind to your silly dog I took her on an adventure with my own dog* is his unstated subtext.

"The seedpod is at least three times as long as her. How did she even fit through the gate with it?" I notice that my tone has become a little shrill.

"Stop worrying. She'll be fine." He disappears back inside the shed, harrumphing.

I make the embarrassing phone call, and plunge right in. "Can you tell me if golden rain tree seed-pods are poisonous, please?"

The woman's voice is warm, concerned. "Has your little one eaten one?"

"Well… um…" I decide on transparency. "Actually, it's my dog. I didn't know who to call…"

She laughs, but with sympathy. "Oh that's okay, I understand. I'll look it up for you." *Thank you God, I actually got an animal lover.*

The news is not good. The seedpods are toxic, and can cause vomiting, convulsions, coma and even death.

She gives me a number to call the Herbarium, to confirm that I've identified the tree correctly. *Cassia fistula.* It sounds even more sinister in Latin.

Next call is the vet. He is relaxed as ever, but becomes more intense when I read out "glycoside function" from my research notes.

"I don't like the sound of that," he says. "But it takes two hours for food to leave their stomachs. Just make her vomit and she should be fine."

"Um… how do I make her vomit?"

"Give her warm salty water. If that doesn't work, bring her down and we'll give her something that will do the trick."

Fifteen minutes later I'm in the car heading for the vet surgery, my clothes drenched, salt drying into crystals on the surface of the fabric. A wet dog wearing a mutinous expression above a still-full tummy sits on the floor on the passenger side. I walk into the vet's waiting room with her, trying not to look panic-stricken. Tom's eyebrows rise a millimetre or two at the sight of our damp and dishevelled appearance, but he wisely says nothing about it.

"How long will it take," I ask as he examines her on the big metal table.

"Not long." He gives me an endless considering look. "Why don't you go home and come back in an hour?"

I stare at him. *Are you crazy? How could I possibly leave her alone with the Grim Reaper circling?*

Clearly this is one of those rare times a man doesn't need an interpreter to know what a woman is thinking. The vet's tone is dry but with an unmistakably firm undercurrent. "We find it's better when their mothers aren't with them."

I drive home again. Ten minutes home, ten minutes back. That leaves forty minutes for pacing and fretting. I'm back in precisely one hour.

The door from the examination room opens, and Tom steps out. His expression is sombre. All the blood drains from my body and tries to escape out my little toe. My mouth is so dry I can hardly speak. "Is she okay?"

Tom's face splits into a grin, and Killarney bursts out the doorway from behind him. She heads straight for me, mouth covered in muck, ears up, tail banner waving.

"Couldn't kill her with a big stick," the vet declares. This is apparently his way of saying her health is strong.

I'm so delighted to cuddle my darling, I don't care that her mouth is covered in muck or even remember to scold the vet for messing with my head. She is fine. She is fine. My puppy is okay.

KILLARNEY AND MACKIE: FRIENDS AT LAST.

Lesson 3:
Joy is having something to lose

ON A HOT SUNDAY MORNING IN DECEMBER, EIGHT-month-old Killarney is yapping – a high-pitched, businesslike noise. She is after something in the wood heap near the barbecue, and she's not playing.

As I run towards her, she is shaking something… something long and sinuous. The ends of it slap against her flanks as she whips it from side to side. She drops it and leaps back, startled, but then plunges in again. In the few seconds it takes me to reach her, it's all over. She looks up at me, panting and grinning, a dead snake lying on the grass beside her. It is a small green snake, shorter than my arm and the thickness of a finger.

"Dad!"

He arrives and gives his verdict. "It's just a tree snake. They're harmless. Put it in the bin. We'll be late for church."

"I'm not touching it."

Dad shakes his head and sighs. He picks it up in a plastic bag and takes it out to the bin.

I'm pretty sure it bit her during the shaking, but I can't find any wounds under her hair. And it *would* happen on a Sunday, when the vet isn't open. I watch her for a while, looking for symptoms of I know not what.

"Belinda! It's time to go!"

Although I love that my new life has brought me back to the church of my childhood, I'm not fully present this week. I sit, stand, sing, sit, and stand for the next hour, but my mind is with Killarney. As we drive back in the gate, my eyes search for her. There she is, dancing a welcome.

By mid-afternoon I have relaxed. She seems fine, and I am languid in the summer heat and humidity. Time for a Sunday afternoon nap.

When the noise starts, it is the same urgent Monster bark I heard this morning. I run outside but I can't see her. "Killarney!"

The noise stops, but she doesn't come. "Killarney!"

I run around the yard, breathing hard. "Killarney, where are you!" I look behind trees and around the odd assortment of sheds decorating the edges of my parents' big yard. "Kill*arn*ey!" Is she *dead*?

I run down the passageway at the side of the

house, and there she is, not limp on the grass but grinning in pride, tail wagging. There is something else "limp on the grass" though. This snake is much bigger. I can't judge the length since she's apparently eaten half of it, but it's thick as a broomstick. That looks too big for a green tree snake. Alarm rises in my throat.

"Dad! Where's the snake book?"

My fingers tremble as I flick through the pages, looking for something green. There's the green tree snake, and it doesn't look quite right. A few more pages and I find another green snake. Fortunately, she's left me the front end, so that I can see the "distinctive black comma" around each eye. It also has a black line across the nose. It is a yellow-faced whip snake, and it's listed in a section titled "Species capable of inflicting severe local symptoms".

"She seems all right," says Dad.

I glare at him, and retrieve the other snake from the wheelie bin. It is already becoming fragrant after a few hours in a hot garden bin, but desperate times call for desperate measures. It has a black comma marking around the eye, and a black line across the nose.

By now, I have Poisons Information on speed dial.

Another pleasant woman answers, and as I tell her my problem I wonder if they've put my phone number on a watch list.

She says, "My information says that it's not particularly dangerous to people, but I can't be sure about a dog. I can give you the number of the emergency vet clinic if you like."

"Yes please."

It turns out to be in a suburb that is a forty-five minute drive away, so I'm in trouble if Killarney needs help. "Keep an eye out for muscle twitching, vomiting or lethargy," says the vet nurse on the other end of the line.

"Are those the symptoms for yellow-faced whip snake?"

"No, that's the symptoms of a tiger snake bite, which is the anti-venom we give for whip snakes." How reassuring. Tiger snakes are one of Australia's most deadly and aggressive creatures in a country spoilt for choice. "It's very expensive though, so we don't give it unless we're very sure it's needed."

So now I have my task as a sunny Sunday afternoon stretches on into night: Dogwatch. I watch her long and hard, but I'm the only one who's twitching. She romps and plays, provoking Mackie as much as she can. She lies down for a rest. Is that lethargy? I poke her, to check. She looks annoyed.

There are more snakes in the weeks that follow. Each time I hear the Monster bark I call her (pointless) and run to stop her (too slow, always too slow). I see the telltale black eye-comma on the limp remains, and move on with my day.

$$\text{\emph{c⌇ɔ}}$$

I'M WORKING LONG HOURS, BUT MY FINANCES ARE STILL sad. After persevering through many weekends of outdoor market research, someone takes pity on me and moves me to a different section, phoning people who've asked to participate in focus group discussions. The days are still long, but I find it much easier talking to people who are hoping I'll phone and offer them money to sit in a room and chat.

I apply for a range of other part-time jobs and become a serial interviewee, but never an employee. Then, thanks to my theology degree, I'm asked to take a part-time role as chaplain at the Conservatorium of Music, Brisbane's music university. Yoghurt has more culture than I do, so being around musicians and composers is yet another lesson in inadequacy. Despite this, the students are gracious enough to let me encourage them, and my horizons widen again.

WHEN SUMMER STORMS COME BLUSTERING IN OFF THE Darling Downs they are hidden by the towering trees until the last minute. Mackie is our early warning system, letting us know he has felt the vibrations of thunder long before our ears can detect them. One day, he skulks off looking for a hidey-hole and I peer through the trees to the southwest. Sure enough, it's looking pretty dark over there.

Killarney is still romping round the yard, and doesn't seem to have received Mackie's advice that we're all about to die.

As rain starts to pound the grass I head for cover, but she runs a few more circuits of the yard, splashing unconcerned through any available puddles. Lightning forks from the sky.

I shout over the noise of the rain, "Killarney! Come out of that weather before you get yourself fried."

She races over to me looking like a skinny rat with her hair plastered to her body. "Well don't you look gorgeous, little puddleduck." She shakes vigorously, sending water all over me as I shriek and laugh. She waggles and grins. Now she has a spiky do, like the strangest all-over gel job.

Next day, I drive back into the carport during another storm, and a wringing wet rat is dancing a welcome at the gate. "Oh you funny little puddleduck." Now that's a nickname that could stick – and it does.

Being Australian, I have to shorten it, so she is variously Puddly, Little Pud, or just Pud. Sitting with her on my lap in the yard one day, I start crooning "You are my Puddly" to the tune of "You are my sunshine". At the end of the first verse it occurs to me to wonder if the neighbours can hear me, and whether or not they think I can hold a tune.

❧

THE SUN SINKS BEHIND THE TREES ON A LONG, HOT Friday in January. The whole world is languid with summer holidays. Killarney starts her Monster bark. It's not a snake this time, but a toad, a big one, and before I can get to her, she's got it in her mouth.

"Killarney! Leave it!" It occurs to me that I'm getting quite good at shrieking. Am I becoming a shrew?

Of course she doesn't leave it. The Call of the Toad is primal and outside the bounds of obedience. I grab the dog and the toad hops away fatly, glistening. Is that poison oozing from its neck glands?

I run to the yard tap with her tucked under my arm, wriggling and protesting. She has toads to chase, but I have other plans for the next thirty minutes. I know from pooches past that I need to irrigate her mouth, letting the water run over her membranes continuously, trying to remove the poison before it enters her bloodstream. Somehow, I have to do it sideways, so she doesn't swallow too much water – let the water flow in one side of the mouth and out the other, rather than down her throat.

She enjoys this about as much as you'd expect.

"Killarney, sit still!" She wriggles and squirms.

I straddle her and then squat down behind her. She is fenced in by my legs, with no way to back out.

I keep it up for the requisite thirty minutes, stopping to give her a break every five minutes. By the end of it, we're both wet through. I'm anxious, and she's annoyed. I watch her for any signs, but she mostly seems to think these water sports are a very odd game, and one she'd rather not play again, thank you. Let's hope it means she won't play with toads again either.

My vet is closed by now, so I call the emergency clinic.

"You've done the right thing," says the voice

down the line. "Keep her cool and calm, and keep an eye on her for a few hours."

"What am I looking for?"

"Seizures, tremors or any kind of shaking."

"She seems all right at the moment. Just a bit subdued."

"That's a function of the poison." *Really? I thought it was a function of having a firehose running through your mouth for half an hour.* "Keep an eye on her, and she should be right."

So, that's my Friday night entertainment scheduled. I'm on Dogwatch again.

♋

I'VE GOT TO GET RID OF THE TOADS. I'M IN GOOD COMPANY with that ambition. Cane toads are killing not just people's pets but native wildlife, and some of the national parks organise evening cane toad control parties. Sometimes they collect hundreds in one night. The buckets of toads are then frozen. Apparently, that's the most humane way to kill them. They just go into hibernation and never wake up.

"You're not putting toads in my freezer." Mum is immoveable on this topic. "They say you can kill them by spraying antiseptic on them. Why don't you try that?"

I potter around the edges of the yard with a spray bottle in one hand, swatting mosquitoes with the other, and dodging the webs of the huge, chunky spiders that inhabit the night.

My targets hop away, but apparently they die later. The next week I find Killarney round the side of the house, gnawing on something.

"What's that you've got?" She looks up at me and I gasp. Between her paws is a dead toad that has dried into a delicious serving of toad jerky.

I pick it up tentatively, using a plastic bag. Another job my arms are not nearly long enough for. Do the poison glands stay toxic?

I call the vet. "Look for salivation," says Hayley. "It happens immediately if they've been poisoned." She tells me that her own dog has been to the stage of glazed eyes and staggering, but no further. "I just sit with her until it passes."

Hayley is a much calmer person than I. But this time at least, Killarney seems fine.

I need a method that doesn't leave dead toads lying around. "Why don't you kill them with a shovel?" someone suggests, as if that is the easiest thing in the world.

It's a horrible thought. But my dog's life is in

danger. Perhaps I can dispatch them humanely with one swift, sharp blow.

This is not a horror novel, so I won't say too much except to hint that big leathery cane toads are not easily dispatched by "one swift, sharp blow".

Growing up in Queensland, hatred of cane toads is almost in a person's DNA. For the first time in my life I realise that it's not this individual toad's fault that it's in the wrong country. It's a living, breathing creature. There has to be a better way.

I stagger inside to drink a reviving cup of tea, pale-faced and shaking. "What about the fridge in the shed?" I say to Mum. It's an old clunker of a fridge that belonged to my grandmother, and the freezer compartment is often near-empty. It has been grinding away noisily there, year after year, chilling dog food and extra drinks for parties.

Mum finally agrees. I grab a marker pen and write "TOADS" and draw big black crosses all over a large empty ice cream container, so there can be no mistake. The plan is to collect the toads in a plastic bag, then put them in the ice cream container and pop them into the freezer for the Big Sleep.

That night I'm out again, but this time I'm wearing yellow rubber gloves and carrying a plastic shopping bag.

I approach my first toad of the evening, and dance around it like a slow-mo prize-fighter, trying to get the best angle. There is no "best angle". I'm going to have to just pick it up. What if it spits at me? I'm pretty sure the "spitting cane toads" thing is an urban myth. *Pretty* sure.

The toad sits stolidly on the grass, thinking toad thoughts.

I lunge in for the grab, but my hands close on thin air. The toad is now under a spiky bush. I spy another, easier mark out in the open.

We do the dance again, but this time my hand comes up with a toad in it. There's nothing slow-mo about the leaping and shrieking that follows – it's more like a deranged karate demonstration. Finally the toad is safely inside the plastic shopping bag. It flops around a few times in there, puzzled. But then it's still. I'm breathing hard, a mix of horror and elation.

At the end of the evening, I've got four large toads in the bag. I put them in the ice cream container, bag and all, and carefully seal the lid. On rubbish collection morning they'll go into the bin – a bag of frozen toadsicles.

I'm exhausted but exhilarated. Finally, a humane solution to my problem. I give Killarney a pat. "I hope you appreciate what I'm doing for you, Little Pud." She waggles.

That summer, I soldier on with the evening Toad Patrol. I get good at it. I stop shrieking about it. One evening I'm on the job when a jogger comes thumping down the roadway just a few metres away. He stops dead, no doubt startled to hear rustling noises and see a shadowy figure in the bushes.

I put on a bright and hearty voice. "It's okay. I'm just on Toad Patrol." *Toad Patrol? How on earth is he supposed to know what that is?*

He laughs nervously and jogs on quickly. He'll have a story to tell his wife when he gets home.

As I seal the lid on my latest catch, I feel good.

I am a brave, fierce dog mother, and I can do things that terrify me if it means I can protect my pup.

GRAND OPENING: KILLARNEY'S NEW DOMAIN.

LESSON 4:
Joy is worth fighting for

THE SAUNA-HEAT OF JANUARY DRAGS ON AND Killarney still walks round the block full throttle. I've heard that dogs can damage their oesophagus if they pull on the leash too hard, but nothing seems to be working among all the advice everyone is so eager to give. She also razzes every other dog we meet, regardless of its size and strength and demeanour – a pint-sized thrill seeker.

I've been making a concerted effort to bond her to me in a multi-dog household, giving her precedence over Mackie in my attentions, and it might have been a mistake. Killarney popped out of the womb with World Domination in her mission statement, and I've inadvertently added to her oversized confidence. If she had a mirror in her kennel, she'd see a giant.

If she spies another dog in the distance, her ears go forward and she gets a glint in her eye. It could be Small Dog Syndrome, except that she's not bluffing. Her assurance is absolute.

The vet says she has "more front than a row of shops". He says it with a grin, but he's not the one trying to keep her out of the jaws of every ill-disciplined four-legged killer in the neighbourhood.

The new school year is starting for the neighbourhood children, and Killarney is going to school too. She *will* be a good doggy citizen.

The beginners' class at the local dog obedience club is full of rabidly lunging dogs of all shapes and sizes. Killarney is only too happy to join the fun – lunging, yapping, and razzing every Rottweiler and bull terrier in sight.

The club uses "check chains". I call them "choke chains", and I hate them. It doesn't seem to matter how adroitly I manage the quick whip of the wrist they teach us. It is supposedly designed to create a sharp "chink" noise as the segments of chain slide over one another. This signals, apparently: "Stop whatever you were about to do." A check chain is meant to be an audible corrective, not a punishment.

Killarney shows no signs of understanding this principle. I think she'd pull on that thing till her head exploded.

I go home exhausted, and then suit up the next Friday evening to try again. There is another Aussie terrier at class and I think, "Great! A cousin for my pup!"

This one has the docked tail of the "breed standard" – which now looks weird to me. Who would do that to an animal when they could have a feathered tail banner telegraphing every emotion to the world? When I tuck her under my arm to carry her somewhere, her tail goes whack-whack-whack against my back. When I approach her when she's in her kennel, I hear a thud-thud-thud of welcome.

Someone tells me the tails were originally docked because Australian terriers were bred to catch rats. When hauling the dog out of a rat hole, it was apparently safer to do so by grabbing the tail where it was thick and strong, near its base – a "handle" of sorts. It's a horrible thought. Surely it must hurt the dog? But then, in the dog pavilion at our annual show I've seen them lifted onto the examination table by collar and tail and the dogs don't seem troubled by it. Who knows?

Killarney's "cousin" has close-cropped hair to go with his close-cropped tail. I don't know if it's been cut for summer heat, or because someone thinks it looks good, but personally I prefer my pup's perpetual bad hair day.

He sits and stands on command, responding to

the slightest flick of the check chain from his handler. He pays little attention to Killarney. His mama looks at Killarney – and me – with disdain. That's okay. I'm not offended. Killarney will probably have him by the throat in a minute, and we'll be even.

Weeks pass. While Killarney will sit and stay when we practise at home, at school she leaps and lunges. The check chain makes her antsy, not obedient.

We come to the end of our first month. Dogs that are performing all the required moves on command are promoted to the next class. We stay in beginners.

A new influx of impossible dogs gives Killarney another invitation to leap and lunge. Across the oval, I see the dogs in higher classes sitting, staying, walking to heel off the leash, and generally showing off. If only a few of them were near Killarney she might copy them instead of the boisterous black Labrador puppy that is currently wrapped around his mother's legs alongside me. He lunges at Killarney, barking madly. She is happy to reciprocate.

The grass needs mowing and it's been raining, so Killarney's undercarriage is sopping wet by the time we leave for home. I'm fighting back tears and feeling like a failure. She's resentful.

Another month ends. Most of the dogs we started with are probably in a show ring somewhere doing somersaults. We are never going to get out of beginners – it's the dog-obedience equivalent of the Hotel California.

As I reverse out of the car park I wind down all the windows to get some air across my heated face, trying not to sob out loud. Killarney has a wild look in her eye. As soon as we're out of earshot of the club grounds I burst into full, unstoppable wailing. All the way home I bellow like a desolate three-year-old. Unlike the melting-eyed terrier who consoled me in my youth, Killarney just looks edgy.

"How was it?" says Mum, before she's noticed my tear-stained face.

"It was horrible. I'm tired of hating my dog. I'm not going back." I throw the despised check chain in a corner where I hope I'll never see it again.

I hurl myself onto my bed to recover from the physical and emotional exhaustion, and try to clear my weeping-blocked sinuses. As I calm down, it dawns on me that with the car windows open my wailing would have been wafting out over the night-quiet streets. My little white car must have sounded like a kind of dysfunctional toy ambulance. No wonder those people at the traffic lights looked at me funny.

Killarney and the neighbours' big mixed-breed dog, Cloud, are conducting a cold war. It causes little real trouble until the day Cloud decides to jump the fence.

I race outside to the sounds of canine bedlam. Cloud has Killarney pinned to the ground. Mackie – stirred either by the thrill of pack behaviour or rebelling against months of having to submit to someone half his size – is joining in the attack.

I shout one dog name after another with very little effect, probably at least partly because they can't hear me over all the barking. By now, Killarney is on her back on the grass, two big dogs on top of her. Killarney's neck is between Cloud's jaws and I'm shrieking like an Oprah audience.

In this incredibly vulnerable position, does Killarney submit? No. She's lying on her back with her neck exposed to two big angry dogs, *giving attitude.*

A thought pops into my head: the handle. I stop shouting and lunge into the melee, reaching for Killarney's tail right down near the base. I grip it firmly and drag her out of there, slipping my other hand under her back as I lift her up and away. Cloud is startled to find her big teeth closing on thin air, but regroups quickly. I hold Killarney as high as I can, while Cloud leaps at an aerial terrier who is *still* yapping and snarling and trying to get free of me so she can rejoin the fray.

The noise has summoned Cloud's owners. They drag her home while I examine my pup, who is bleeding around the neck but thankfully only from surface wounds, nothing serious.

The worst of it is, I'm pretty sure Killarney thinks she *won*.

ᔐ

ANOTHER NEIGHBOUR HAS A HUNTING DOG NAMED Gerald. When I say "hunting dog", I don't mean "hunting breed", although he is a ridgeback. I mean a dog taken into the outback to work in the culling of the dangerous feral boars that infest some parts of Australia. I would never go near Gerald without his owner present, and I don't think I've ever touched him, although he's a beautiful animal.

One day I'm returning from a walk with Killarney when I see Gerald's dad in his front yard. I stop for a chat, and as Killarney walks near to Gerald I'm glad there's a reliable fence between the two of them and a strong man on hand in case of any ensuing chaos when she razzes the wrong dog.

My eyes open wide as I watch her. There is not the tiniest sign of aggression. She wiggles along the fence beside Gerald who looks down his nose with gracious condescension. Her expression could best be described as coy, and I swear she's fluttering her eyelashes. Apparently, my little nutbag can recognise a true Alpha Dog when she sees one.

☙

DAD NEEDS HIS TRAILER BACK AND KILLARNEY IS NEAR adult size, so her kennel is relocated to the dog housing estate under the guava tree, next to Mackie's kennel. She must be tied up to it for the full toading hours from dusk to sunrise.

When I'm going to be out during tie-up time, I nag my parents before I leave. "You won't forget to tie her up before dusk, will you?" Dad in particular shows a displeasing lack of hysteria when it comes to my dog.

☙

I'M HOME ALONE IN MUM AND DAD'S BIG HOUSE, ON their big block of tree-clad land with the neighbours just a little more than a scream away. My parents are travelling, visiting friends and family interstate. The house creaks and shifts and makes all kinds of alarming noises. I read until much too late, but finally turn out the light. Quite a bit later, I drop off to a restless sleep.

The Monster bark wakes me. It's two o'clock in the morning.

I'm instantly awake and out of bed, torch in hand. Heart pounding, I creep to the back window, peering out to try to see what shadowy villain Killarney is warning off, and hoping whoever it is can't see *me*.

Oh. It seems she's after something on the ground, not something at burglar-height.

I flick on the floodlight that turns half the backyard into daytime. She's after a toad.

Half an hour later, the whole mouth-irrigation charade over, I dry myself off and bring Killarney and her basket inside. I'll be on Dogwatch until at least 3.00 am, so I'm breaking the "outdoor dogs" rule. I'm sure my parents would understand if they were home.

❧

"Dad, what if we built a run for Killarney? We could put something around it to make it toadproof."

"We?" He has a point. I'm not at all handy when it comes to home improvements.

"Well, you. But I'll pay for the materials. And I'll help you."

My vision is for a world where I can put Killarney to bed at night and know she's safe. And if we're all going to be out after dark, whoever is last to leave can put her in there before they go, and not have to worry about her. It will be the security of the trailer-castle in a much more durable format.

He scratches his beard and ponders it for a while as though he might say no, but the fact is, my Dad likes to build things. An engineer never really retires.

It becomes a huge event, like lots of my Dad's projects. Anything my Dad builds stays built. He draws up his designs, and I pay for fencing materials and paving that he selects. I do get a choice about the colour of the paving blocks, so that's something.

The partial roof to give Killarney some shade outside her kennel will be a piece of corrugated steel that Dad already had slotted neatly away in his comprehensive collection of Useful Things.

We work together on the construction, although my contribution is token at best. Still, it feels good to work on something with my dad.

The pavers are perfectly laid. They are surrounded

by chain link fencing overlaid with chicken wire, because toads can oozle through chain link. Chicken wire extensions prevent toadly inveiglement around or under the gate.

We hold a grand opening ceremony, and take a photo. Killarney's kennel is placed in position, and she is introduced to her new domain.

She is one year old and already well aware that the world revolves around her, so she takes this new proof of her humans' devotion in her stride.

At sunset, I shut her into her pen and blow her a kiss through the gate: kiss-kiss, blow. She lifts her chin abruptly to sniff the movement of air from my mouth, and it looks for all the world like she's "catching the kiss". I settle down that night for the most relaxed sleep I've had in ages.

ℰᴖ

ON THE THURSDAY BEFORE EASTER, I ARRIVE HOME from work in the dark wondering if I'll find Killarney desolate from my many hours of absence, but she's belting around the backyard at her customary one hundred miles per hour. She and Mackie are "having a rumble". Every so often they catch each other and tussle on the grass, accompanied by lots of high-pitched yapping and the occasional deeper woof.

She is half Mackie's height, which complicates the canine intimidation procedures, but only slightly. Instead of looking down and away to indicate his submission when she bosses him around, Mackie looks up and away. He now spends quite a lot of his life with his neck in this awkward position.

"Why isn't she in her pen?" I say to Dad.

"She's fine. There's no toads now."

We're six weeks into autumn, so it's possibly true, although I'd rather not take the chance. But something about her gait seems strange.

"Killarney!" She comes to me, does a little dance, and looks fine. *Must be imagining it.* I give her a pat, but she's not interested in staying long. She takes off for a victory lap of the yard.

This time, I'm absolutely certain she's limping. I call her again and wrestle her into a firm grip. "Show me your paw." Her look says: *Are you kidding? I want to run.*

It is another learning experience for me. I discover that dogs really *really* don't like having their paws handled. When I can finally get enough light on the subject, I can see that her front paw is about twice normal size. The pads are puffed up so much that the claws have almost disappeared. I groan. It is

Thursday night at the beginning of a four-day long weekend, so my regular vet won't be available.

What if it's infected? A memory skitters through my mind about a former work colleague who spent a week in hospital near death, all because of an infected finger. Infection in the extremities shouldn't be ignored.

I dial the emergency vet near the inner city, many suburbs away. They confirm that infection could be a problem. "Watch her for a while."

At eleven thirty pm the foot is still enormous. I'm exhausted. I dread the long drive to the city on my own. I look at Dad. "Will you come with me?"

"Yes, I'll come with you." My hero. He doesn't even sigh in frustration, although I'm sure there are plenty of things he'd rather do in the middle of the night, such as go to sleep.

The nurse at the emergency clinic turns out to be someone I went to school with a thousand years ago – no mean feat in a city of two million people. While I wait for the vet, we chat and catch up on the intervening years. She has children to talk about, but of course I can only mention a dog. My life has been full and rich, but this is one of those moments of regret.

In the small hours of the morning, we drive home.

My credit card is lighter by far too many dollars, and I have a detailed list of instructions for the foot. The diagnosis is allergy, not infection, so it could have waited a day or two. And the likely culprit is cement dust from the pavers in Killarney's new pen.

In the dark, we move her kennel out of the pen, and get her set up under the guava tree again.

The next day, I hose the cement pavers with the full force of water, hoping to remove as much of the dust as possible. I do it again. And again.

After it has dried, we put Killarney back in there. The next day her paw is puffy.

We move the kennel out again.

On Dad's instructions, I buy a pot of concrete sealer from the hardware store. When I get home and offer it to him, he hands me a paintbrush from his collection, gives me a few tips, smiles and walks away.

I can do this. I crouch down on my knees to paint the clear sealant over the paving tiles. Occasionally I forget and straighten up and brain myself on the low-hanging roof. I stagger around for a while clutching my head, and then resume painting, headachy from the head bashing and the fumes.

When the second coat is fully dry, we move the kennel back in again.

Her paw puffs up.

We move the kennel out again.

I'm beginning to feel desperate and Dad's eyebrows are drawing together in one dark line. He spent a lot of his precious time and energy building that beautiful pen.

We discover a piece of linoleum in Dad's collection of useful things. Cut to size it becomes the new floor of her pen, obscuring those perfectly aligned beautifully-coloured concrete tiles.

Kennel and dog are moved back in. We wait, but the paw doesn't puff. We thank God for old lino and unpuffed paws.

RUSSIAN STRAYS, OR ANGELS IN DISGUISE?

LESSON 5:
Joy is unpredictable

THE MILLENNIUM BUG IS IN THE NEWS. WILL ALL the world's computers collapse at the stroke of midnight on December 31? Other debates swirl around whether it really *is* the new millennium, or if that should begin in 2001.

My mind is focused on simpler problems. I stand in front of a shop full of evening dresses and chew my lip. Hang it. I've got no money but I'm going inside to try something on.

Some of my friends prefer to just greet the new year in the morning, but I've got a drop of Scottish blood and my family has always watched midnight tick over.

Even as a young child, I recall being woken in the middle of the night to drink a homemade chocolate milkshake. Then I would lie down and go back to sleep – a puzzling event and yet a tasty milkshake. The smallest of five children learns early that if a treat is offered, it's best consumed quickly. Years later the thought struck me, "Oh, that must have been New Year."

But a new year means far more to me than special snacks. As that clock ticks over a door opens, a portal to anything and everything. I am a lifelong Pollyanna. No matter how many times I'm disappointed, I always think maybe this will be the year – the year I find my life partner, the year I finally write my novel, the year I get an amazing job, the year of great things. And this New Year will be extra special.

I look at my reflection in the mirror, an elegant stranger in a floor length dark red sleeveless number with discreet diamantes around the v-neck. The slinky fabric drapes along every curve – including a bit of a tummy I'm pretty sure wasn't there a couple of years ago. The salesgirl flicks a dismissive hand. "It's all about the underwear," she says.

I hand over my credit card, and head off to the underwear shop. And then I go home and await the invitations. A swanky party would be nice. Or even a refined dinner party. But no invitations come, and I flounder around trying to organise something myself. It seems as though every friend and family member in my address book is keeping their options open, just in case they get a better offer.

December 31st dawns and still I have no plans. My beautiful dress hangs limp and silent in the wardrobe. One redeeming feature of the season is that a friend from Sydney has come to stay a few days, so at least my parents and I will have more than just each other to look at.

"Why don't we go out for some coffee and cake?" says Mum. She likes to be around a critical mass of humans at New Year, same as I do.

We shut Mackie and Killarney in the shed rather than just their kennels, because there are bound to be illegal backyard fireworks this year. We make them a nice nest, so they'll have protection from noise, and not be able to run away and get injured on the road if they get alarmed.

"Fill the baths with water," says Dad. "Then we can use it to flush the toilets if the water goes off." He worked in local government, so he's aware of the role computers play in vital infrastructure.

"What about some saucepans of water for drinking?" I ask.

"Yes, good."

We unplug all the appliances from the wall in case of a power surge. And we head out to a nice restaurant. But they close at eleven pm.

Disgruntled, we move on to a low-key gathering

at our church, where we encounter a gaggle of other New Millennium refugees playing board games. We say "Happy New Year" to one another, sing Auld Lang Syne, and then go outside expecting to see the thrilling spectacle of street lights snuffed out, satellites falling from the sky, and looting in the streets. However, apart from some high-pitched toots from party whistles a few streets away, nothing happens. The Millennium Bug turns out to be the most successful false marketing scheme of all time.

My fears of neighbouring fireworks, however, were not so groundless. As I let Killarney and Mackie out of the shed, they are panting and looking a little wild about the eyes. *I just hope she doesn't get scared of loud noises after this.*

ᏸ

I WALK OVER DESERTED SAND DUNES AND PAUSE TO GAZE at the ocean turning silver in the dusk. I can almost taste the cool, salty breeze. I become aware that I'm not alone, and turn to see another sea-inspector, a man about my age, just as he notices me.

Don't panic, he's not a roving axe murderer. We're wearing matching nametags.

I say, "It looks like we're attending the same conference."

He smiles. "Are you enjoying it?"

We discuss the keynote speaker, and then, even though with the nametags it's not strictly necessary, I say, "I'm Belinda, by the way."

"I'm Callum." His handshake is firm, his eyes a warm brown. He is altogether tall, dark and handsome.

We talk for longer than necessary. He is witty and good with words. He drops enough into the conversation for me to suspect that he is single. I'm about to leave the country for several months, which suddenly seems like very bad timing.

I mention my destination in eastern Europe, where I have agreed to help a publisher who is translating historical documents into English. "A few people have asked me to keep them up to date. I'll probably send an email newsletter every few weeks."

"That sounds interesting," says Callum. "Let me give you my email address."

ᕱᕱ

IN THE BLISTERING HEAT OF EARLY FEBRUARY I BOARD A plane headed for the blistering cold of regional Russia. Killarney, approaching her second birthday, is in the care of my generous built-in petsitters again.

In a city of millions I manage to connect with a very small handful of other ex-pats from around the world, and meet with them whenever I can for the opportunity of speaking my native language. I discover how many dialectic differences our language has! But we muddle through, and it is at least more successful than my attempts to communicate in the local language. Sometimes I am invited to ex-pat homes, where I edge around the piles of bottled water they accumulated in preparedness for the Russian infrastructure collapse certain to occur when the clock struck 2000. They are gradually drinking their way through the stockpile.

In a Brisbane summer there's no way to purchase clothes that are equal to a Russian winter, but one of the ex-pats lends me her spare overcoat and I fold away the inadequate parka I arrived in, deeply grateful. Her spare coat is a puffy synthetic number with a hood, coloured a glaringly-bright royal blue in a city of elegant fur-lined neutrals. I look like the result of a match between a Smurf and the Michelin Man, but I'm warm. I buy fur-lined boots, but they are nothing like the Ugg boots I wear at my desk in the winters at home. They are gleaming black leather with a fashionable heel, because that is all I can get. They are the biggest available and yet at least four sizes too small for me. I would have expected Russian women to be tall and athletic, but at only 170 cm (5' 7") I am a giant, looming over the local women like a big blundering blue tower.

The local diet, in winter at least, seems to involve mostly grain porridge, some dairy – including the world's best sour cream, not much meat, and rarely any fresh vegetables. Fruit is for birthdays only. I am sobered by the discovery and make a mental note to give thanks more often for the lavish abundance of my home country. My clothes grow tighter thanks to the fatty diet and the chocolate bars I buy every time I feel lost and lonely, but I have no full-length mirror and can't see the full disaster unfolding.

The city is filled with rows of dismal grey Soviet-era apartment blocks, but the homes within them are surprisingly warm and bright. Footpaths are rarely cleared of snow, and become icy and hazardous. I use the sharp edges on the heels of my boots like ice picks, trying oh-so-hard to stay upright. One ex-pat tells me, "Have you noticed the number of amputees? That's how they treat a compound fracture here." Is it true? I don't know, but I ask friends back home to pray that I don't fall on the ice.

I rent a room in the tiny apartment of a gregarious local woman. She practises her beginner-English lessons with me while I stumble through basic Russian, over meals of rice and fatty meat, or for breakfast, Napoleon cake and stewed tea. We have earnest conversations about the weather, because there is a lot of it, and we have words for it. She finds me a puzzling creature because of times like the morning the thermometer outside the window glass announces −25C and I throw on my outdoor clothes and race downstairs just to know what −25C feels like. (It feels cold.)

ᛜᛜ

I SEND OFF MY FIRST EMAIL NEWSLETTER TO THE FOLKS at home, and Callum is on that list. On impulse, emboldened by distance, I fire off a personal follow-up to Callum, but I keep it very short – a quick thank you for a bon voyage message I'd received from him.

A reply comes back the same day. It too is short, but friendly. A steady exchange develops, and the emails get longer. He tells witticisms about goings-on at his work. I recount stories about a Brazilian soap opera dubbed into Russian that I watch during dinner where everyone is weeping, including most of the men, and my landlady tries to explain the plot using her ten words of English.

Our conversation topics deepen. I'm home alone one day and feeling bleak about my career. I write it all down in an email to Callum.

"I'm thirty-six, supposedly in my prime. I should be settled and focused, with solid achievements behind me. Instead I have nothing to be proud of in the world's terms. (Although I do have some very nice stamps in my passport…) Sure, I know that Someone has it all in control ultimately, and I do trust him, ultimately, but in the face of the everyday grind, I get confused. People I sat beside at press conferences in the early eighties are now foreign correspondents in Moscow or New York. I got fed up with TV, because I realised TV news wasn't really about news, it was about personalities and backstabbing and being superstars and asking grief-stricken women whose sons had just been eaten by crocodiles, "How do you feel?" So I got off the roundabout in 1988, and went off to work for a Christian organisation for a pittance, never to be seen again. One newspaper I write for is pleased with my stuff, but they don't see me sitting paralysed at my desk, willing myself to pick up the phone and call an interviewee."

A long reply comes back:

"I hate being categorised by age or anything else for that matter. The world is good at telling us we're too young or too old. What is the right age? Glad life's not like that movie Logan's Run where you get put down on your thirtieth birthday. What you're doing now has a purpose. Have you considered that perhaps no one else could do what you are doing? I haven't known you for long, but it's clear you do a fine Belinda Pollard."

As I continue to muddle through each day's struggle to communicate with the locals, I start to live for Callum's emails. When I dial in and there's nothing from him, I'm crestfallen. But when his name pops up in my Inbox, my heart leaps.

ↁↂ

MY LANDLADY NEEDS HER ROOM BACK FOR ANOTHER booking. When I move to a different apartment, my new landlady speaks no English and finds my attempts at Russian baffling and possibly insulting.

But she has a satellite dish. One day when she is out, I happen onto Animal Planet. Television in English! Better yet, there are dogs. I watch enthralled as Lassie tries to announce with a few well-timed barks that Timmy is stuck down the well. Good girl that she is, she doesn't give up until she convinces them, and Timmy is saved.

The credits roll up the screen and another program

begins about a veterinary practice – set in Australia! Dogs *and* familiar Australian accents. I go "aww" over a quivering spaniel on the big metal table. His problem is diagnosed, he goes home healed, and I smile. Then there's another segment, and the vet is out on a house call. Horror of horrors, she is putting someone's dear old dog to sleep, in the familiarity of his home. It is all done with great compassion and affection, but by the end I'm sobbing. *I might have to do that for Killarney one day. I wonder if Tom makes house calls for such a task. Yes, my dog is only two, but it's going to happen someday.* Thankfully, I've managed to stop weeping by the time my landlady gets home – can you imagine trying to explain that one with a Russian-English dictionary as your only aid? But I fear my eyes are still a little red.

Mum studiously learned how to operate my computer before I left Australia. She has a long list of step-by-step instructions that she follows to the letter. My mother is highly intelligent, but incredibly busy. She often doesn't bother with a subject or verb in her sentences, because who has time for that and I'll understand her meaning anyway. Her regular news is therefore a lot shorter than Callum's, but it's full of goings-on among people I recognise and love, and it's a treat.

But there is no way to connect with my dog. During one of our rare and expensive phone conversations Mum says, "Do you want to say hello to Killarney?"

She holds the phone down near the dog. I say, "Hello Puddly. How's my girl?"

Muffled noises follow before Mum comes back on the line. "Oh no! She's running everywhere looking for you." We don't do that again.

A space between my apartment block and the street holds a scraggle of winter-bare trees and some abandoned, tumbledown houses built of dark timber. A pack of dogs live in the ruins. A lot of the stray dogs here are a mixture of shapes, colours and sizes – a gathering, rather than a breeding set. But this group has some members of the same family. They are a similar size to Killarney, with coarse, scruffy fur.

An ex-pat tells me that some people had no alternative but to dump their pets when the economy became so bad. Many people are not even receiving their government pension. There are the usual beggars around this kind of city, but also proud little old ladies sitting on benches with one hand out, eyes averted. During a two am stop on an overnight train trip, I peer out the window as people with crystal chandeliers and enormous vases in their arms walk up and down the platform, stopping and spruiking as windows open, eager to make a sale. I'm told that their employer, a crystal factory, has no money, so they pay their staff in crystal.

Their stories break my heart, and I give coins now and then but there is so little I can do to make a real difference for anyone. If I had children who were reduced to only two meals of grain porridge a day, I wonder how I would care for Killarney. There are no pet shelters, here. No alternatives. I'm sure these dogs in front of my apartment building were loved by humans, once upon a time. But their owners had to let them loose in a different part of the city and hope they'd find a way to survive.

And somehow, they are surviving. People stream past them all day, but I never see anyone pay them the slightest attention, not even to scold. The relationship appears to be mutual. They interact with each other and their environment as though the humans don't exist. But I begin talking to them as I walk past, for some kind of contact with a dog. I don't attempt to touch them nor do I have any food to give them. I just murmur a greeting to them – in

English, mostly, with occasional faltering words of Russian. It's probably not entirely surprising that while I struggle to recall my language lessons, the word for "dog" – *sobaka* – has stuck in my memory. I mutter the endearment form of it, "Hello *so-batch-ka*", and click my tongue. I do it quietly so that other pedestrians can't hear me.

At first the dogs ignore me like they ignore everyone else. One day, the alpha dog makes eye contact from under his scruffy eyebrows, then looks away. The next day, he holds the contact longer, and a couple of others walk forward to look at me as well. Weeks pass, and somehow they are coming out from the ruins to greet me each time I walk past. There is no jumping or dancing like Killarney might do. It is a reserved greeting, just a lifted head and a slight movement of the tail, like the small smile-and-nod that business associates might exchange as they pass in a corridor. I'm not going to be there long enough to do anything useful for them, but their acknowledgement of my existence lifts my spirits in a way that's hard to describe. In a world where you're out of place and no one understands your conversation, the acceptance of a dog is a precious thing.

❦

IT IS NINE O'CLOCK ON A MOONLESS NIGHT, AND SNOW IS crunching under my fur-lined boots as I head up a deserted street into the darkness. Two young men got off the tram at my stop. They are drunk and belligerent, and they are following me. They are calling out in a leering tone what may be insults or come-ons or threats. Perhaps all they are shouting is, "You look stupid in that Michelin Man overcoat." But I doubt it.

Little do they know their verbal ingenuity is wasted on me. I can't understand a word. But menace is an international language.

My pulse must have hit about three hundred and sixty beats per minute by now. I focus my attention on walking and breathing. There is still enough light for me to see my breath clouding in the air in front of me, but the street is getting darker, metre by metre, and it is lined with blank-faced apartment buildings. Soon I will have to turn off towards my building and navigate the long, dark, narrow laneway between the hulks of the old timber houses. The path I must walk is lumpy, uneven, and slick with ice. The security door at the base of my staircase has a combination lock. *What are the numbers again? 4927? 4297?* Each mistake with the code entry requires a reset, and I don't have time for that.

"There isn't a lot of random crime in this city." That's what one of the ex-pats told me. Apparently, you have to be a drug dealer or connected to the local mafia to see the city's seamier side. I hope I'm not about to become the exception that proves that particular rule. I'm praying continually and incoherently under my breath, "Please God, help me!"

The two men are gaining on me. Their shouts are louder, their voices singsong and rough. I reach the laneway and there's nowhere else to go, so I plunge into that dark opening, moving fast, my breath catching in my throat.

The men are close behind when pandemonium erupts. My family of stray dogs bursts from under the old, broken house. They stream around me and straight past me to hurl themselves at the men, barking with furious intent. Chaos reigns behind me, but I don't look back. The men are still shouting but their tone is now one of panic.

Two more minutes and I'm inside the building, leaning on the door and trembling with relief. *Thank you thank you thank you.* As the tears start it occurs to me that guardian angels come in many different shapes and sizes.

A MODEL OF GOOD BEHAVIOUR.

LESSON 6:
Joy is embracing your own uniqueness

ARRIVING BACK HOME IN BRISBANE, I CAN'T WAIT TO see Killarney. I am greeted with silence. She stands stock-still and stares. I wonder if she has forgotten me in four short months. I shrivel just a little inside.

But then she starts running. She does a circuit of the yard, comes back, does another circuit, comes back and then does another circuit. I unshrivel, and try to pat her on one of her fly-bys, laughing.

I am also eager to see Callum again, be in the same room with him, go on some dates and be normal. But it's undercut by nerves. Will we gel, in person? Or are we just pen pals?

I meet him. He smiles. I smile. I've got a hunch he doesn't know what to do either. A handshake would be ludicrous, after all the things we've shared. In the end we settle on a brief, platonic hug.

I struggle with reverse culture shock. I read car number plates as though they are the Cyrillic alphabet and sometimes find myself about to answer a question in Russian – a language that had deserted me during many an exchange when I actually needed it. I can't believe I own so many things, that our shops are so crammed with fruits and vegetables so many colours of the rainbow, that we waste so much, that we have the temerity to own land and yet not use it to grow our own food.

None of my clothes fit me after several months of the world's best sour cream and I go on a crash diet because I can't afford to buy new clothes. All my life I've had a racehorse metabolism, stick thin no matter what I ate or how many cruel "skinny jokes" people made about me. Now in my mid thirties it seems to have shifted into low gear and after years of wishing for some fat on my bones I don't know who this pudgy stranger is who has borrowed my skin without permission. I go to the charity shop to get a few garments to tide me over.

Dates with Callum are sporadic, weeks apart. To me, this is not what a flourishing relationship looks like. Should I just call the whole thing off? Months pass, and it's like we're marking time. I wonder if fear of commitment will end up being the main thing we have in common.

But I love my dog. And she loves me. She

organises a parade in my honour every time I come home. She's a social butterfly who loves everybody, but at the top of her list is me. She doesn't care if I'm not pretty enough or poorly dressed or too emotional or tell too many corny jokes. Killarney will never reject me.

හ

THE PHONE RINGS OUT OF THE BLUE AND IT'S A MAN I'VE never met called Michael from Christian Television Australia (CTA). He's heard about me somehow via the network of relationships I still have with various segments of the media.

"I hear you've worked in television," he says. "The producer for one of our shows is taking six week's leave and I need someone to fill in for her. Are you interested?"

"I'm a journalist and I've worked in television, but I'm not a producer."

He replies, "I'd rather have a journalist who's not a producer than a producer who's not a journalist. It's easier to teach someone production than 'news sense'."

It's a national weekly magazine-style program called World View, discussing significant events and popular culture. It's put together on a shoestring budget. CTA is a production company rather than a television station. It is donation-supported, so the money won't be very posh. World View broadcasts at six o'clock Sunday mornings on one of the big Australian networks. Michael tells me how Channel Nine donate air time, studio time, editing time and even the footage from their news library partly as a way to fulfil legislative requirements to include a percentage of religious content, but really because someone high up the chain of command is very generous to specialist groups. I won't be required to present anything, which is good because I'm not feeling very photogenic. I will write a lot of scripts, run the show and do the voiceover for one of the segments.

In no time, it seems I have committed to do this thing. Michael turns out to be around my age with a journalism background and the whip-smart verbal humour I've encountered so often in journalists, tempered by kindness. He is clearly proud of his five daughters, referring to them as "the netball team".

Stacey, the producer, is a young and chirpy woman with great attention to detail. She explains that we are given an editing slot in the television newsroom after the evening news has gone to air on Friday nights, when much of the station is dark and silent.

On a good week I might expect to get out as early as eleven o'clock, but Stacey warns me she has been there till the early hours of the morning on many occasions.

I shadow her for two weeks in an attempt to become her mini-me on very short notice. As we're preparing the rundown for my first "week in review" segment, the radio news playing in the background announces a disastrous fire at a backpackers hostel in Central Queensland. I used to work in a nearby city in the eighties and I'm shocked that something so awful has happened in such a quiet and beautiful country town. But I'll have to be sad later. Stacey and I look at each other with both gravity and certainty. "There's our lead." I haven't worked in hard news for over a decade, but I find that I automatically know what to do next. It's like putting on a favourite pair of old forgotten shoes and discovering they fit every contour of my feet.

I meet the production team at Channel Nine, and enjoy the sardonic humour flying around the darkened control room as the program unfolds on the studio floor below us. As producer, I have my own monitor to watch, a volunteer running the autocue, and a clutch of scripts to manage as we pull all the segments together. World View is recorded

"live to tape" – no editing – the day before broad-
cast. Michael is executive producer and therefore
my boss; he is also the presenter of this particular
program in the CTA stable, so when he's in front of
the camera I'm *his* boss. It could be a complex relationship, but it seems to flow with simplicity and
harmony each week, untainted by the egos and am-
bitions that disrupted my television work before.

When Stacey decides to resign at the end of the
year to head in a different direction with her career,
it's no hardship for me to say yes to the invitation to
take her place permanently.

ↅↄ

MY LIFE IS EXPANDING AND CONTRACTING IN VARIOUS
directions. Callum and I finally have "the talk". The
clearest I have ever been about the shape of our relationship is the day we agree that it is over. I feel
as though I've wasted a year of my life. But mostly
I just feel sad.

Meanwhile, the platonic section of my social life
is booming.

The annual round of Christmas parties is bigger
due to the projects I've been involved in, especially
with CTA. At one of them I meet another journalist,
an elegant blonde woman a little older than I am.

Her name is Lauren. We talk shop for ages, souveniring hot nibblies from platters as they go past and generally ignoring the other guests. It's a joy to meet someone who knows how you think – the cynicism of journalism with the optimism of faith.

"So you're with CTA," Lauren says. "I've been wanting to do some volunteering with them."

I take her card. "That's great. I'm going to need someone to look after guests next year."

⁕

AFTER THE NEW MILLENNIUM DEBACLE, I'M DETERMINED 2001 will be welcomed in a better style. There's no trouble choosing a theme, and so invitations go out for "2001: A Space Oddity".

My family have a long history of weird costume parties. In fact, I went to my own twenty-first birthday party as a Lipton's tea bag. I was a baby journalist at the time, so the chosen theme was "celebrities and scribes". My father came as Pat McEnbrat in homage to the tennis-court tantrums of Pat Cash and John McEnroe, carrying a broken tennis racket, wearing a wild wig constrained by a headband and a Davis Cup t-shirt I received as a freebie while unaccountably covering Sport for my radio station. My sister and I attended as Pot Strength and Cup

Strength, with huge to-scale teabag tags created by my sister bearing the Lipton brand and the slogan "famous throughout the world".

For 2001: A Space Oddity, Dad wheels out the glow-in-the-dark life-size spaceship scenery he created for a physical culture concert back in the 70s when the older girls danced to Carole King's "I feel the earth move". He positions it so that people have to enter our house through the spaceship door. They are impressed, assuming we've created it specially. They clearly don't know the power of a good shed.

Mum and Dad are Martians, with green face paint and bobbing antennae.

A friend turns up as Arthur Dent from *Hitchhiker's Guide to the Galaxy*, wearing pyjamas bearing the number forty-two. I ask him where his towel is, but he doesn't understand the question, so I fear it must be a while since he read it. (If you haven't read *Hitchhiker*, you won't understand it either. Go read it, and report back to me.)

There are several Star Trek characters who have clearly spent money at an actual costume shop, and they keep asking what my costume is.

"I'm a space oddity." I'm wearing a fluoro purple Cleopatra wig, false eyelashes, an orange tutu and hiking boots. They look puzzled. You just can't help some people.

It's a smaller party than the ones of my youth – it turns out that New Year is a hard time to get post-moderns to commit, especially when my parents have insisted on a "no alcohol" rule. But it's fun and we've launched 2001 with a bang instead of a whimper, and that's good enough for me.

ↄ

IN A MATTER OF WEEKS, I'M IN THE HOT SEAT WITH CTA as we develop a new panel discussion segment. Lauren is there to organise our guests as they arrive – guiding them through security, supervising them through makeup, keeping them calm while they await their turn on the set. She is a natural for the task.

I have already discovered that she is a cat person, but it becomes a point of connection rather than difference because it turns out she's as invested in her animals as I am. She invites me to lunch at her elegant home after taping one hot Saturday, and I finally meet the moggies. Caramel is a fluffy mix the colour of warm honey with a personality to match. Once she gets over her shyness, she even wants to be stroked.

The second cat, a sleek nearly-black Siamese, is a different matter. "You need to be careful with Cocoa," Lauren says. "He's on anti-depressants, and he can be a bit strange."

For some reason, crazy-cat takes a shine to me. He winds around my legs, purring like a machine gun. I sense that claws are an option he's keeping in his toolkit as I reach down tentatively to touch him. He submits to it, rubs his head against my hand three times, and then stalks off like a supermodel on crack. I breathe a sigh of relief that I have survived unperforated. But I'm secretly pleased to be chosen. Being chosen by a dog is wonderful. Being chosen by a cat is a miracle.

CHRISTMAS BELLE.

Lesson 7:
Joy is having flexible expectations

"I THINK I MIGHT BUY A HOUSE," I TELL MY PARENTS. "It will be a savings account with a roof on it." Dad nods in approval. I'm thirty-seven and my Dad thinks it's high time I started acting like a grown-up.

The government is offering a grant to first home buyers: $14,000 if it's a new build. They're trying to boost the economy. For years I've spent any left-over money on travel and I've moved house more times than I can count. But is this a good time of my life to put down some roots? I don't have to stay in the house forever. I could always rent it out and take off overseas for a year or two.

Over the next few months I hop in and out of the cars of different real estate agents, looking at the cheapest houses on their list. Whatever I get, it has to be manageable by one not-very-handy woman, and it has to be dog-friendly, with a way to provide toad control.

My dream house is a restored "Queenslander" on

acreage. This is a traditional timber house named for my Australian state, raised on leggy stumps so the air (or, sometimes, floodwaters) can circulate underneath, with high ceilings and wide, shady verandas. Its corrugated iron roof amplifies the pounding of summer rain – a lullaby I recognise from childhood. It's a house built to make the most of every precious cooling breeze in a steamy sub-tropical climate. When and if the temperature change finally comes through during the night, the timbers of these old houses murmur the stories of the families who have walked their boards for generations.

Well, that's my dream.

My reality is something else. I view a series of horrible, squat little houses. I don't mind small. "Big house" just means more cleaning to me. But I do mind dark and dingy.

I finally reconcile myself to the fact that all I can afford is a townhouse – one small dwelling in a group, with community rules, and managers who take care of the common lawns and gardens. I'm not at all opposed to having my lawn mown by someone else, but the thought of having to abide by a long list of regulations horrifies me. "So you want to build a turret on the roof and paint it lime green? Sorry. No can do." I console myself with the thought that my neighbours won't be able to build a lime green turret either.

So next I view a series of depressing little townhouses with poky kitchens and dark walls. I have always been willing to make the most of an uninspiring dwelling in my many previous moves – one flat I rented didn't even have a kitchen, so I cooked in a microwave and electric frypan, washing dishes in the bathroom basin – but buying one is harder. Some of the courtyards barely seem bigger than my parents' old dining table. How happy will Killarney be in that? "Just think of it as a savings account with a roof on it," I remind myself, and try to be sensible.

There's one townhouse village nearby that I haven't really considered. It's down the end of a road to nowhere. After lunch with my sister one day she says, "I really think you should go and have a look at them."

As we drive up the street, that song about little boxes made of ticky-tacky is going through my head. A new stage of the village is under construction and close to completion. A workman says, "You should talk to Don."

Don turns out to be the developer of the complex, a kind-faced middle-aged man. "I've only got one left," Don says. "Do you want to have a look inside?"

I walk through the front door, sceptical, and am met by a big, bright open space. The kitchen is full-sized. The two bedrooms are both big enough for a queen-sized bed – either would make a spacious home office. The garage has a remote control door, so that a person getting home from work at one in the morning could be inside the house before they ever had to get out of the car.

I step out the back door under the shelter of a steel pergola which provides a roof for about a third of a huge courtyard. I see a good spot for Killarney's kennel. Beyond the paling fence lies parkland and even a creek leading to the river I glimpse in the distance – the acreage I've dreamed of, in a different form.

Have you ever walked into a house and unexpectedly felt at home? Yeah, that.

Dad the Engineer comes to view it and declares it soundly built. He takes me to the local authority offices so we can check planning proposals and flood maps, and it is cleared of any guilt in that department. Roadblocks melt away. I can't afford it; the bank increases my loan amount without blinking. Don the developer leaves a few non-essential items out as they complete the build, so he can charge me a few thousand less. I really wanted the one with the courtyard that faces northeast where our summer breezes and winter sunshine come from but it is already sold; Don persuades that villa's purchaser, an investor who doesn't plan to live in it, to switch villas with me. I feel as though God is giving me this house. I have no idea why I should be the recipient of such generosity, and it makes me thoughtful and thankful.

Killarney and I move into our new home one chilly July day when the ducks from what is now our local pond are just beginning to go out on dates. Soon there will be ducklings around, joining us in our own new phase of life.

ဆ

WE INTERVIEW THE AUTHOR PHILIP YANCEY FOR WORLD View, and I'm a little star struck. He owns a section of my bookshelf. I even hand him my favourite, *Reaching for the Invisible God*, and ask him to sign it. As a young journalist I was trying so hard to fit in I never asked for an autograph from anyone I interviewed. I've finally given up trying to be cool.

Yancey writes beautifully, but it's more than that. He isn't afraid to tackle the big, troubling questions of human existence. He is a journalist making a difference with his words. Oh how I wish I could do something like that.

One of my clients, a UK publisher I write Bible meditations for, asks me to produce a book. I become a "published author" which is lovely, and it's wonderful if anyone is helped by it, but I still somehow hanker for my novel. I don't know why I want to do something so frivolous when there are much more "worthy" opportunities on the table. Some days, I don't really know who I am at all.

ఴ

KILLARNEY IS AN OUTDOOR DOG AT OUR NEW HOME, JUST as she was at my parents' house. One of my brothers says with a smug smile and a knowing look, "She'll be inside in no time. Just you wait and see."

How ridiculous. What would he know?

I do, however, give her a chance for a quick peek. She's not used to being inside and gets excited and nervous, dashing from room to room. The master bedroom has a full-length mirror on the wardrobe door, and Killarney has never seen a mirror before.

She careens into the room and yaps in shock, leaping up and back at the sight of another dog. She darts back and forth, lunges towards the glass for a quick confrontation but then thinks better of it and heads back out of the room. She doesn't engage this other dog in full battle, but perhaps that's because it doesn't seem like a dog that would be easily intimidated.

I have had to sign all sorts of things to allow me to have a dog in the village, and I'm nervous. *What if she's a nuisance and they make me get rid of her? I'll have to move out if she can't stay. I don't want to be here without my dog.* Every time she looks like even thinking of yapping, I jump on her and silence her. "Shush, Killarney," I whisper-shout. She starts to become a much quieter dog.

Dad comes over with his tool belt to help me set up the courtyard to be a larger alternative to Killarney's pen at his place. He selects stainless steel mesh in a small square grid pattern, and we work together attaching it to the fence to fortify the gaps between the palings. Like all Dad's construction efforts, it's built to last.

There's the possibility of a toad climbing up the drain, so the top of that is covered with mesh, too.

Fort Killarney is established.

As Dad is about to leave, he says to Killarney, "Come here and I'll give you a scruffle." She trots up to him expectantly, and he takes her head between both big hands and vigorously rubs her face. She staggers a little and her blonde wisps emerge an even bigger mess than usual, but she seems pleased with the tough love. Perhaps she's missing him too.

I develop my own farewell routine with Killarney. Each time I leave the house I "blow her a kiss". I bend down, she looks up and we go through the kiss-kiss-blow charade. It becomes our signal that I'm going out and, this time, she's not coming. She's very relaxed about taking sole charge of her fortress.

As the weather warms into summer, we get a few days of rain and humidity. I arrive home in the dark from a long day at work and greet my dog. She comes forth from her kennel, leaps with joy and greets me royally.

A slight movement catches my attention in the dim light beyond the kennel. It's a baby cane toad, not much bigger than my thumbnail.

"Oh no!" I race inside for a pair of rubber gloves, race back out and grab the toadlet. I'm not sure what to do with it since the Big Sleep is not really an option in my kitchen freezer. I weigh it in my hand a moment then shrug and put it over the fence.

And then I see another movement. And another.

I gasp. The courtyard is alive with baby toads.

Phase Two of Fort Killarney takes place the

following weekend. I buy metres of synthetic shade cloth and Dad comes over to help me attach it to the fence with a staple gun. It's an eccentric decorative touch in my splendid new courtyard, but the Frankenfence will just have to be a feature. A beautiful outlook won't be much comfort if I can't separate my terrier from deadly critters.

℘

AMONG MY NEW NEIGHBOURS IS A FRIENDLY YOUNG COUPLE. They have a beefy English bulldog named Winston, who is not really any taller than Killarney but about as wide across the shoulders as she is long, and it's all muscle.

As I drive in one day with Killarney in the car, I notice Russell from next door, so I stop in the driveway and hop out to say hello. I haven't seen that Winston is with him, but Killarney has. She leaps out the door I unwittingly left open, and it's on.

Winston has a relatively staid personality but he doesn't take kindly to her yelling in his face. He's not wearing a leash and he plunges in with a deep roof-roof-roof and a look of serious intent. Russell is standing back looking dazed.

Killarney is about to become dinner for one cranky bulldog, so I grab her by the handle and pull her out of there, hoisting her into the air with my other hand under her chest.

She scrabbles at me, scratching my arms in her eagerness to get down and show Winston who's boss, still barking her head off. Russell says a couple of ineffectual things to Winston, who is now climbing my legs, and I can report that a heavyset bulldog is *heavy*set. His claws leave painful train-track welts down my knees which should mature into an interesting set of bruises later.

Winston's dad finally enters the melee to drag Winston off me, and I head into the house to deposit my still-furiously-yapping terrier. I come back out to conclude my chat with Russell, trying to look nonchalant. After all, I want to keep in good standing with my new neighbours. My bruised legs are throbbing and there are tiny beads of blood on some of my arm scratches, but I pretend all is fine.

We finish our chat and I go to put my car in the garage, but there's a bulldog in my seat. I can't even imagine how he was able to get up there on such short legs.

"Oh yeah," says Russell with a nod. "He loves going in the car." Clearly, Winston doesn't much mind whose car it is. Russell doesn't seem to mind, either.

"Come on Winston," I say. "Out you get." *And get your dusty paws off my sheepskin seat covers while you're at it. I don't even let my own dog on those seat covers!*

Winston shows no sign of having heard me. I try to shift him, but between his great weight and great determination it's like trying to move a monolith. Winston stays sat, unmoved and unmoving, head tilted up so he can almost see over the dash, tongue lolling happily. "Um… I can't get him out."

"Oh, right," says Russell. He ambles over and gets his arms around Winston, trying a couple of different angles. Even his big muscles strain with the weight of the animal, but finally Winston is outside my car, looking disappointed.

"See you later," I say, pasting on a bright smile as I head off to wash my wounds. I'll need to do a Winston-check each time I take Killarney out walking in the future.

ೞ

KILLARNEY AND WINSTON LEARN TO GET ALONG, GRUDGingly, either side of five-foot tall pickets. Whoever said "good fences make good neighbours" must have had Killarney and Winston in mind. Some days there is a little light growling at the gaps in the fence, sometimes a little snuffling, but mostly they appear happy to ignore each other.

The parkland over my back fence is undeveloped – just a nature reserve really. It lies alongside paddocks that actually contain cattle, an enduring pocket of farmland in the urban sprawl. Don the developer keeps the park mown because it presents a nice backdrop to the new stage of the village he's building.

It is perfect for walking Killarney. We wander and she sniffs, ears up, eyes bright. After a few walks, since there's no one in sight I take the risk of letting her off the leash. She runs full of the joy of freedom but she keeps circling back to me, just to be sure. At the end of the walk she returns happily to have her leash clipped to her collar again.

One sunny day she heads off into the longer grass near the creek. "Killarney! Come out of there. There might be ticks."

She romps back to me, leaping over the long, springy saltwater grass. She stops and circles back, sniffing. Something has her nasally occupied in the grass, and I can't see what it is. The next moment she hurls herself down on her back and wriggles and writhes in pure canine delight.

She eventually emerges from the grass, but her

stink precedes her. Obviously there was something dead in there.

"Oh, Killarney!" Her odour is at Defcon Five and it's a challenge for me even to venture close enough to reattach her leash. She prances home to a personal theme song along the lines of "I feel pretty". Little does she know that disappointment awaits. As soon as we get inside she's going in the laundry tub for an immediate bath.

❧

KILLARNEY'S EARS GO FORWARD IN HER STALKING POSE – she's seen a large group of ducks. She makes a sudden charge and ten ducks take flight all at once. They stream past low overhead and Killarney follows in hot pursuit. "Killarney!" She reaches the barbed wire fence at the edge of the park and slips straight through underneath it into the farmer's paddock. "Kill*arn*ey!" Still the ducks fly and Killarney runs. She's through the second barbed wire fence. *"Killarney!"*

There are cattle in the second paddock, and Killarney has never seen a cow before. She hasn't seen this one, either, until a big white mountain in her range of vision *moves*. Even a giant among dogs won't take on something that many times her size.

She hits the brakes, stopping more suddenly and completely than I've ever seen a fast-moving object stop.

But now she can't find me. The grass is too long, she's too far away, and Australian terriers don't have very good distance vision. I call her name over and over while she jumps vertically in the air, front paws up like a rabbit, trying to see me. Once she's got a lock on my direction she comes belting back. I clip her leash to her collar, where it will be staying during all future walks.

I go on the hunt for a long retractable leash. At the pet shop they are $36, which is outrageous. I find one in the $2 shop. "Bargain!" On our third walk with it, she sees something interesting and goes racing off. As she hits the full extent of the leash, the connection snaps and it flies back and hits me in the face not far from my eye. Once I've got Killarney back under my control and mopped up the blood, I reflect that some bargains come at too high a price. I go back to the pet shop and buy the $36 version.

❧

NESTING PLOVERS PRESENT A NEW THREAT. GROUND breeders, they lay their eggs in the middle of a footpath and then become outraged if people walk by.

They attack in breeding pairs, circling at altitude before swooping from different directions. I become accustomed to the sound of their warning cries – staccato and high-pitched. It is my signal to take Killarney home. Being a terrier who looks at the ground Killarney barely notices them, and given her high self-esteem probably wouldn't care if she did. But I care. "They have spurs on their claws," people tell me in hushed tones.

We are a long walk from home one afternoon when I hear the warning sound. Killarney is out at the full extent of her leash and I call her to me. She looks at me, waggles, and thinks I am just being sociable. Plover A comes in for a long low bombing run, guns firing, uk-uk-uk. "Kill*arn*ey! *Come!*"

She starts trotting towards me as the bird swoops just above her head. Surely she at least felt the breeze of it rushing by? But she's still grinning and relaxed.

Plover B is now banking to the left so he can come at us from the north. I break into a run, dragging Killarney behind me up the hill at the other end of five metres of cord. She stumbles and loses her footing, hurtling along behind me like an out-of-control waterskier, as Plover A engages missile lock from the west.

I don't stop running until I'm inside the comparative safety of a path between two houses. I stop to catch my breath and look back at Killarney. She's on her feet again and wondering what this new running-dragging game is. Beyond her I notice several workmen lined up along the edge of the building site, watching the whole thing. They're probably concerned for my safety, so I give them a nonchalant wave. "It's all right. I'm okay!"

Their hoots of raucous laughter waft out over the parkland.

RARE SIGHTING: TERRIER AT REST.

LESSON 8:
Joy is making the best of life's imperfections

SUMMER SLOUCHES INTO BRISBANE, AND IT'S THE hottest we've had in years. When the World View season ends for the summer break, I'm stuck in my home office all week far from the refuge of air-conditioning. Around Christmas, the maximum temperatures are above 40C (104F). Humidity slides off the windows. I'm trying to edit books, but I can hardly think. I take cold showers four times a day. I stand in front of a pedestal fan wafting my shirt up and down so the breeze can cool my stomach. I take out my bank statement and calculate just how long it might take me to save enough money to install air-conditioning.

Summer heat means summer storms with ferocious winds, pounding rain and sometimes hail. I'm relaxing with a cup of tea in the courtyard under the steel-roofed pergola one afternoon as the sky darkens ominously. Killarney is sitting at my feet. The first few big drops fall: bang, bang, bang-bang. And then it starts. The rain thumps onto the thin metal roof, and I revel in the sound of it. The wind is blowing so hard the rain is almost horizontal, but it's okay. It's blowing away from me across the courtyard and into the parkland, and I'm safe and dry under the pergola.

But then I realise if it's blowing away from me at the back of the house, it is hitting the front of the house straight on. The front of the house where I left a big window open earlier. My eyes pop open wide and I shriek as I stand and run. Killarney runs after me, barking her head off. Curtains are blowing at me and I try to get around them as I stand on the wet carpet and wrangle the window closed. I'm laughing now as I go looking for towels to mop up the mess, but a glance at Killarney shows me that she is panting and anxious.

As weeks and months pass, Killarney becomes ever more fearful of storms and loud noises. The fireworks of the previous New Year had begun something, my alarming storm-reaction developed it, and the wide-open spaces of our new home are finishing the work. Before, tall trees hid the full scope of a storm from Killarney's low-altitude viewpoint. Now she is able to see both sheet lightning and ground strikes through our fence as storms lash the river floodplain. We have a much bigger sky at this house, and it can be a very scary sky for a small dog.

She runs around wild-eyed and barking in storms now, and tries to wedge herself between her kennel and the wall. When I have air-conditioning installed, the compressor becomes yet another thing she tries to crawl behind. Even indoors she's not happy, turning into a perpetual motion machine trying to wedge herself into small gaps behind furniture. If I wasn't there to extricate her, she could easily electrocute herself in some of the wires behind appliances.

It breaks my heart and I don't know what to do about it. Everyone has advice. One well-meaning friend says, "Put her in the laundry. That's what we always did with our dog." That's not much help, and not only because I don't have a laundry. Most of our worst storms hit at a time of day when I'm not home to put her in a laundry or anywhere else. I have to find a way to give her the life skill of finding safety on her own, and it's a responsibility I'd rather escape if I could. Her robust kennel is the safest place of all, if only she would get in there instead of running around terrified in the wind and lightning.

When a storm hits in the middle of the night, I bring her inside hoping she'll feel safer and settle, but she keeps roaming. I'm exhausted and decide to lie down and see what she'll do. My eyes open to rummaging noises. Killarney is directly beneath me, tunnelling under my bed. I'd happily leave her there even though she's officially not allowed in the bedroom, but she doesn't stop. She forges a way through the shoeboxes commando-style, and comes out the other side tangled in power cords and dust bunnies. Then she comes back round to do it all over again.

I begin a training program where I leash her at her kennel during storms, hoping she'll learn it's a good place. I peek from behind the furniture to see what she's doing, and eventually she hops into her kennel to wait it out. I'm relieved and hopeful, but when I come home after another storm she's wet again, so she's not doing it when I'm not there.

Some nights during storms I bring her basket into my bedroom and leash her to the bed leg beside me. That stops the tunnelling, and she eventually settles down in one spot, panting. The problem seems endless, and I breathe a sigh of relief when the weather cools into autumn and the storm season is past for another year. My carefree dog is back until summer comes round again.

I'M STILL DOING A MIX OF WORK FOR DIFFERENT CLIENTS, but CTA production takes up a big chunk of the week for nine months of the year. Several nights a week, I don't get home until after dark. Killarney enjoys romping in her great big courtyard all day whether I'm there or not. She has never been a dog to feel insecure or lonely. But I say to myself, "What's the point of having a dog if I never see her?"

And so she becomes an indoor-outdoor dog. Arriving home at night, I open the sliding door and she sits obediently, looking intently at me till I give the signal that she can come in. I buy a wicker basket for her so she can curl up beside me while I watch television. She comes in for a few hours after dinner each night, whether I'm working at home or in a client's office.

She learns some of the new routines of being indoors with her mother. I'm always losing track of the cordless phone handset, so when it rings and I run round the house, she runs with me from room to room, barking and leaping with the thrill of the moment.

I'm not a sports lover, but I do like to watch the annual State of Origin, a rather brutal series of football matches between Queensland and our southern neighbour, New South Wales. When the score line gets stressful, I'm inclined to jump up and shout. Killarney is pleased to join in.

❧

KILLARNEY IS FOUR WHEN MACKIE BECOMES ILL. HE IS getting old. The vet isn't sure what ails him, and Dad frowns if I ask about the dog. One day Dad comes home to find that Mackie has departed quietly, on his own terms and in his own time.

After we say our goodbyes, Dad says, "I don't think we'll get another dog. We want to travel more and it will be easier."

Killarney gets a lot more scruffles from her grandfather after that.

❧

KILLARNEY MIGHT NOT LIKE MANY DOGS, BUT SHE LOVES humans. When visitors arrive at my house, she revels in greeting her public.

She develops an unfailing ability to hunt out the one in the crowd who does *not* like dogs, and sits on that person's foot. She settles down under the dining table when I entertain. She never gets fed from the table – she just loves humans around her.

A foot-sniffer, she likes to press her damp nose against people's ankles and feet. Even a dog lover grows tired of this pretty quickly, but for some dog unlovers who come for lunch I have to take serious measures, shutting her outside the screen door to give them some relief.

Winter arrives, and I take the bold step of inviting the CTA staff and their families to my home for Sunday lunch. I cook roast beef with crispy potatoes, lavish amounts of bright vegetables and my mother's special gravy, and cram twelve chairs around my new dining table, bought from the Special Deals room at Ikea. It needs both its extensions to cope with this job. Killarney is outside for the meal because there are just too many legs in a small space and she would become a trip hazard.

Michael, my boss, stares at her in amazement as she sits at the open door, watching us. "How do you stop her coming in?" he says. "I could never get my dog to do that." I think of his leaping Labrador puppy and feel pleased that Killarney has turned into a very obedient dog. It's a big turnaround after all those horrific obedience classes that I've buried in the Trauma pocket of my memory. Maybe I'm not such a bad dog owner after all.

It's a holiday long weekend, so after I've dealt with all the dishes from my guests, I join my parents at their shed in the hills about an hour from home. It's a simple steel construction with several beds, a table and a wood-burning stove all in one big room. There is no electricity and the mobile phone coverage is poor, but it does have a flushing toilet.

In summer it's a challenge to get far enough away from the heat radiating out of the stove as it cools from the cooking task. But on a bitter winter night it's bliss to sit around it reading as the gas lamps hiss. Killarney is tucked up in her basket outside the door, sound asleep. I'm reminded of Buttons, one of the dogs of my youth, who looked quite a lot like Killarney and also enjoyed her visits to the shed. Buttons used to fetch cowpats and curl up in her basket with these treasures, in exactly the same location.

The shed is on a five-acre hill, and it's Killarney's first visit without Mackie. They used to race around it freely until the time Mackie came back from a solo visit covered in hundreds and hundreds of ticks, confounding even the vet. In the end, the only feasible treatment was to put Mackie through a cattle dip

– traumatic for all. Since then, Killarney is either on a leash, or running on the mown section and being called back before she hits the long grass. I feel sad that she has to submit to this restriction, but ticks can be deadly. Even with the restricted movement, I fret and check her diligently from head to toe. So far I've only found one on her belly, before it got fully engorged. Rather than being saddened by the curtailment of her enjoyment of the big block, Killarney leaps and waggles and grins the whole time she's there.

The next day is bright with winter sunshine, and we set off with Mum and Dad for a long walk around the hills. Killarney trots along beside me on her leash, behaving like the perfect dog she has become. We pass one property where a middle-aged couple are out gardening and we start chatting. Beside them, a miniature black poodle is rolling in the grass.

The woman looks at Killarney and says, "Oh, I'll let Peppy out and they can play together!"

"Um… no… don't do that." But it's too late. She can't hear me, and wouldn't understand if she could.

Peppy comes flying down towards Killarney. Killarney goes flying up towards Peppy, teeth bared and growling, pulling at the full extent of her leash.

A brief skirmish follows, concluded by Peppy tearing back up the hill to the safety of his own gate. The woman is now glaring at Killarney, and the atmosphere has become distinctly chilly.

Killarney's three humans slink off with our tails between our legs, metaphorically speaking. There's nothing metaphorical about Killarney's tail. She is waving it high, broadcasting that she is queen of all she surveys. I recall how smug I was about her behaviour only twenty-four hours previously and reflect: pride cometh before a fall.

❧

SOMETIMES MY BUILT-IN PETSITTERS ARE NOT AVAILABLE, and so I have to find a boarding kennel – not a straightforward task when you've got a dog-razzing, cane-toad-chasing pet.

I'm recalling the reliable boarding kennels we sometimes used in my youth so when I have to go to a conference while my parents are away, I naively make a booking at a kennel I find in the Yellow Pages, once they assure me they'll do their best to keep her from toads. I arrive to find it's surrounded by bushland. I can barely hear myself think over the barking and yelping. A man with a brusque manner takes Killarney's collar off and hands it to me.

"That way we won't lose it." He tucks her under his arm and walks off as I stand watching with my mouth open.

I don't know if this is normal or what else to do, so I leave. She comes home alive, but is deranged for about a week.

The second attempt yields a glamorous "pet resort" with manicured grounds. Killarney piddles in the reception room on arrival and it's all downhill from there. The woman in charge tears strips off me and my dog management abilities. She at least seems to like animals, so I leave the dog in her care and drive off in a quiet rage.

My third strike finally produces a home run. It's a relaxed suburban boarding kennel, not posh but not awful either, run by an elderly couple who adore dogs. The prices are cheap, and I have a hunch when I collect Killarney that she has been in their house at least some of the time. She agrees to come home with me, but either way would be fine with her.

Sadly, the elderly couple eventually decide to retire and sell up. The new manager is a middle-aged woman with a warm, no-nonsense manner. She lets the dogs run around together in a big yard, instead of locked up in their own run.

"Killarney doesn't get on so well with other dogs," I warn.

"We find they settle down when their owners are not around and they don't have to protect their territory."

"Um… well I hope so… it's just that, well—"

"We should never be embarrassed by our dogs." She gives me a stern look.

I drive off, feeling rebuked.

On my return, the manager gives me a smile that is just slightly tight on the corners. "She's got quite a strong personality, hasn't she?"

℘

KILLARNEY IS FOUR YEARS OLD WHEN I FIND A LUMP ON her stomach near a nipple. It's small, but distinct.

The vet feels it. He doesn't look anxious. "Let's keep an eye on it for a few weeks."

A few weeks later it's still there, and it seems slightly larger to me. But then it's hard to be sure when you're checking it every day.

"We probably should take it out."

I blanch. Surgery. I've heard of dogs dying in surgery, refusing to wake from anaesthetic.

I'm given a surgery date and strict instructions.

I'm to bath her the day before, and she's to have no food or water after midnight.

"I'm working the day before. What should I do?"

"Bath her when you get home at night."

Oh. Killarney seems to find the concept as odd as I do when I put her in the laundry tub in the evening. She doesn't like it at the best of times, but to drench a dog in the cool of the evening seems particularly bad form. I towel her dry, but it's not enough.

I dig out my hairdryer from the back of the bathroom cupboard and stare at it. I hardly ever use it because it only seems to turn my natural curls into a frizz-bomb. Can you blow-dry a dog? My Dad, who washes his dogs in the garden, would be horrified.

I show it to Killarney and turn it on so she can hear the loud noise. She skitters away through the house.

I use my sweetest voice. "Killa-a-arney." She prances back into the bathroom. I direct the drier at her flank for a moment. She skitters away, but then she comes back and runs in front of me so I'll do it again. We play the hairdryer hokey pokey until she's Dry Enough.

The next morning I deliver her into Hayley's care, trying to look calm and positive for the sake of my dog. "She'll be fine," says Hayley kindly. "You can phone about three o'clock to see how it's gone."

"Um, do you mind if I give her a kiss before I go. It's this thing I do and it will, um, let her know she's staying here and it's okay."

"Sure." Hayley has obviously heard a lot of things in her time in pet care.

I blow the dog a kiss, Killarney catches it, and I walk out of the vet office with a red face.

I struggle to concentrate all day, and shoot an email to Lauren about my fears, since she's one friend I know will understand. My habit when I'm stressed or worried is to take it to God, but I'm not sure about the theology of praying for pets. God has a lot bigger issues on his plate than one little dog.

"I pray for my pets," replies Lauren.

I send up a few tentative prayers as the day drags on, and I wait till 3.01 pm to pick up the phone, because I don't want to look *too* eager.

"It went well," Tom says. "We got the whole lump out. Lots of dogs have these and live to be fifteen. Just let us know if you find any more lumps."

ﭏ

KILLARNEY IS RESTORED TO HER CANINE CANNONBALL status within a day or two, long before her stitches even come out. It takes me a little longer to get over it.

When I find the next lump, I'm slightly less scared, since it went well the last time. By the third lump, I know the drill.

It seems like annual surgery might become part of our life, and I rearrange my headspace around that idea. Killarney keeps running, her enthusiasm for life undented.

Small dog, big heart.

LESSON 9:
Joy can't get through if we're obsessed with misery

THE MONSTER BARK WAKES ME AT A DISGUSTING hour on a Sunday morning. I stagger to the window and peer out, bleary-eyed. Early sunshine is streaming across the courtyard, and Killarney is attacking something behind a pot plant. Probably just another snake. She'll wake the whole village with her racket. "Killarney!" She ignores me.

I run outside. "Killarney!" The snake is inside the base of a self-watering pot, and she can't get a clear shot at it. She pulls back sharply and then darts in to snap at it, then pulls back again. Her bark becomes more angry.

Eventually, the battle is over, and the snake is in two pieces. It's only small, a baby really. I examine it and feel my stomach shift as I realise it isn't like any she's caught before. It's a copper-bronze colour. Its belly is cream with orange flecks.

I pick up the phone and look at the clock. Only six thirty. But I need to know.

"Hello?" a sleepy voice says.

"Dad, can you get the snake book please?"

While he's finding the book, I call her and she comes to me. Was that a wobble in her step? I'm not sure.

I try to describe the snake while Dad flicks pages at the other end of the line. Killarney walks into the corner of the courtyard, right in under a spreading shrub. She starts vomiting, a deep, dry heaving, and then falls flat on her belly, her chin thrust forward and resting on the ground, completely still.

"Dad, I'll have to hang up and call the vet! She's collapsed!"

I dial the vet's home number with rubbery fingers. Killarney is not moving. Is she dead, so fast?

The phone rings out. The vet could be asleep. He could be away. But I don't know what else to do, and so I call the number again. It rings out and I dial it again. Finally, a woman answers. I hope I've been dialling the right number!

"I'm sorry to bother you so early. Is this the vet's phone?"

"Yes, but he's asleep at the moment." She is polite but a little distant.

"My dog's just been bitten by a snake. She's collapsed." My tongue is so dry it's like trying to talk with a pair of rolled-up socks in my mouth.

The woman's voice becomes warmer. "Is she still breathing?"

"I'm not sure. I can't tell." My voice catches on the words, and I draw in a slow breath to try to steady myself. "I'm sorry, I'll try to be sensible." For some reason, it's important to me not to sound like the Crazy Lady just now.

Tom comes on the line as I'm crawling in under the shrubbery, trying to reach the dog. I can't get at her properly and I have the phone in one hand anyway, so I have to pull at her. Her hairy little body drags across the garden bed like a sack of sago pudding, her chin bump-bump-bumping across the ground. I'm sure she's already dead, but when I get her onto the concrete, there is a flicker of life.

"I'll meet you at the surgery," Tom says. "Bring the snake."

I call my parents as I'm racing inside to get changed, so they'll know what's happening. A quick change into a cotton house-dress, a quick dash to the loo. While I'm washing my hands I glance in the mirror to discover that I look like the Joker's sister or a deranged panda. I'd been too lazy to remove my makeup last night and it's now awash with tears. I pause long enough to grab a bottle and a cotton ball to remove the worst of it. I'm not sure why I'm bothering, since my hair looks like a shrub after a storm and it's going to stay that way.

I scoop up my darling little dog and race to the car. She lies limply on the floor on the passenger side, while I drive through quiet Sunday-morning streets. Part of my route goes through a pocket of farmland, and there are no cars around so I press down on the accelerator.

Theological debates are cast aside and I pray in earnest, tears coursing down my face. "Please God, save her. Please God, don't let my puppy die." Between gear changes I reach down to touch her and hopefully give her comfort, still watching the road. Out of the corner of my eye I see her head lift and sway, but then she collapses back down onto the floor.

Within fifteen minutes of the phone call, I'm standing outside the vet's plate glass sliding door as he unlocks it from inside.

"Put her on the floor and let me see how she is."

I place her carefully, and she sags to the ground. At that moment, Mum and Dad arrive. They've ob-viously come to offer moral support because they think I'm about to need it, and I can't imagine how they've got here so fast.

Killarney sees them and everything shifts. She gets up and totters over to them, eager to greet two of her favourite people. Her tail wags and she dances around.

"Let's just watch her for a while," Tom says. He examines the dead snake. "She might not have been bitten. The young snakes aren't supposed to have venom yet. And the anti-venom can kill a dog anyway, so we don't give it unless we have to."

Four adults sit on chairs around the edge of the waiting room, while Killarney holds court. She is chirpy and cheeky, unrecognisable from the sago-pudding-dog of half an hour ago.

"She looks okay," Tom says. "Take her home and keep an eye on her."

Mum and Dad offer to follow me home and keep me company for a while. Less than two hundred metres down the road, Killarney starts heaving again, and collapses onto the floor of the car.

I pull over, and my parents pull over behind me. I get out my mobile phone. "She's vomiting again," I tell the vet.

"Just take her home and keep her quiet and watch

her for half an hour. Then call me and let me know how she is."

After the longest half hour of my life, I call Tom, and in another fifteen minutes we're all back for a reunion at the vet surgery. Tom takes one look at her lying limply in my arms, nods, and leads the way into the examination room.

I put Killarney on the big metal table and hold her close as she sags against me, eyes glazed. Tom lays the snake out on the bench, poring over its markings and comparing it to charts and books. "It's important to identify them correctly so we give the right anti-venom," he says. "You have to count the scales. It looks like it's an eastern brown."

He shaves her furry foreleg, prepares the anti-venom, and looks me in the eye. "The anti-venom is dangerous. It could kill her, so we don't give it unless she's at more risk without it. I have to give it a bit at a time, and watch for a reaction. I need you to hold her very still while the needle is in her leg. Can you do that?"

I'm terrified. I can't stand the sight of blood. I hate sickness and hospitals. "Yes, I can do it." With no vet nurse present on this Sunday morning emergency callout, I'm the only one available. I put on my calm face, wrap my arms under and around my puppy and hold her perfectly still as the vet begins to inject the potion that could kill her or save her.

He depresses the syringe a fraction, and watches Killarney. The clock on the wall ticks loudly. He must be satisfied with what he sees, because he depresses the syringe another tiny fraction. Again we wait. My shoulders are beginning to cramp with hunching in this strange position for so long. Her blood, thin and watery, is flowing over my forearm from the injection site. I make soft clicking noises with my tongue. "That's a good girl," I murmur. "Good girl, Killarney."

I don't know if it's been hours or minutes, but eventually the syringe is empty. Still we watch. She looks slightly less dead.

"We'll take her out to the waiting room and watch her a while," Tom says.

"She bled all over me," I say absently, holding out my arm for his inspection.

"That's what the venom does."

I'm startled. I hadn't thought of that. I look at it and wonder if that means I've got snake venom on my arm.

He sends me to a sink in a room out the back so I can wash it off. I've never been in this part of the vet practice, and it feels strangely exclusive. He shows me where to find a towel. There's blood on my dress too, but I'll worry about that later.

Outside in the world, the city is coming to life and people are doing Sunday things. In the waiting room, we sit with Killarney as the morning creeps on, and gradually she comes back into her eyes from wherever she'd gone. She is weak and doddery, but she is alive.

 confirm

With Killarney stabilised and very quiet, she is sent home with me to rest and recover.

"Just watch her and let me know if you're concerned," says Tom.

"What am I looking for?"

"Flat dog." Well, that's specific. So apparently she could still collapse, even after all we've been through to save her.

And so she rests while I watch. I go online and look up eastern brown snakes. The Queensland Museum website says its other name is "common brown snake". Common as in there's lots of them. The venom is "strongly neurotoxic and haemotoxic; the second most toxic land snake venom known". The snake has a "pugnacious" temperament.

I learn that they breed around rivers and creeks.

I peer over my back fence at the creek in the distance and the outlet for the stormwater drain just a few metres away. I live in an eastern brown snake nursery.

Never again will I be able to casually dismiss the Monster bark.

We get through the first day, and Killarney trudges around the house trying to summon up the occasional waggle. I stare at her with big eyes. What am I going to do? Her instincts are so strong. If she survives this disaster – and she hasn't survived it yet – how can I ever keep her from biting another deadly snake?

Days pass, and I spend hours online looking for suggestions. What I find is a lot of other disaster stories that make me anxious. Someone spent $3000 rescuing their dog from a brown snake bite. "She was never the same again," they say. People discuss wild schemes for trying to keep snakes out of a yard.

I put her to bed each night in her basket just near my bedroom, so I can keep an ear on her through the night. I hammer a hook into the skirting board so she can be leashed there, as she finds it confusing to be in the house when I'm not up and about. That way she rests well because she knows where she is meant to be, and I rest better too knowing that at least she can't get any snakes during the hours of sleep.

Some forums I read kick around the idea of Vitamin C injections as an emergency all-purpose antidote to snakebite if you can't get anti-venom. I wonder where I could get some injectable Vitamin C and how I would store it. Turns out Vitamin C injections go off. And what do I know about giving injections anyway? What if I injected it into the wrong place and killed her?

Someone else says they gave Vitamin C in the weeks after their dog was bitten, and it seemed to help with the recovery. I've got some Vitamin C powder that I put in my morning juice in the winter. I stare at the label, and then at the dog. I sprinkle a little on Killarney's next meal and wait to see what will happen. It doesn't seem to make her sick, so I keep doing it.

I roam around online, clicking links, being horrified, becoming obsessed. Killarney is slowly picking up, but the light seems to have gone out of her eyes and I don't know if it will ever come back. When I close my own eyes at night, I can see those words "she was never the same again". It is the Christmas season, and I hate leaving her alone to go to celebrations. I never know if she'll be there to greet me on my return.

Days turn into weeks, and I find a spray online that is supposed to deter snakes by interfering with some special sense of smell snakes apparently have. *What have I got to lose?* I order a bottle and spray it liberally around my boundaries and along the gap under the garage door. It stinks to high heaven. I'm not sure what the snakes think of it, but it certainly repels *me*. I spray it every few days, and freshen it up after rain. I live in a fog of snake repellent.

There are also solar-powered thingies that supposedly emit some kind of vibration disturbing to snakes. The reviews are patchy, and I figure a funny noise might not be so good for a dog, either, so I resist the urge to buy those.

If I hear Killarney barking, I rush out to see what it is. What if a snake has just left after giving her a quick nip? I look for evidence of staggering gait or dilated pupils. She finds this especially annoying at night, when her pupils are naturally dilated. I shine a torch in her eyes to see if the pupils contract. Any uncertainty, and I give her some Vitamin C. She becomes the most anti-oxidated dog in Brisbane.

Killarney begins to enjoy life again, but I don't. Every time I arrive home from work I take a few deep breaths and steel myself for the possibility she'll be lying dead in the courtyard.

She isn't the kind of dog who can be indoors full-time – she's had freedom all her life. She likes to be out in the fresh air. I don't have a doggy door, and even if I installed one it would serve as a snake superhighway directly into my dining room.

Dad and I apply ourselves to the problem of how to snake-proof the courtyard gate. Nothing we try works well enough and still allows the gate to open and close. I spray more snake repellent.

I look it up online and apparently snakes can flatten themselves and do some kind of Houdini trick of getting themselves through tiny gaps. I look at the gaps in my fence and despair. I spray more snake repellent and give Killarney a little more Vitamin C.

People say brown snakes can't climb. Then I meet someone who says they saw a brown snake get a fright and go straight up the inside wall of their house, right alongside the washing machine, and then into a hole in the ceiling. Up a sheer plasterboard wall, not a textured one.

"Are you sure it was an eastern brown snake? Lots of snakes look brown."

"It was a brown snake. Trust me."

I think of the snake-scaring mower that trundles

past my fence. I spray more snake repellent. I add Vitamin C permanently to Killarney's breakfast.

Killarney grows stronger by the day, and her immunity is rock-solid with all that Vitamin C, but I barely notice. I'm on Snake Alert 24/7.

BRIDGET MAYHEM, SHOWING AN
EARLY APTITUDE FOR TEXTILES.

LESSON 10:

Joy is a new way of looking at things

MEANWHILE, IN OTHER NEWS FROM THE WORLD outside Snake Central, I eventually notice that Dad is missing having a dog.

"I'd like to give you a puppy for your birthday if you'd like one," I say. "You don't have to give me an answer today. Just think about it."

Dad scratches his mass of curly grey hair and looks at me sideways.

A few days later I say, "What sort of dog would you like if you got one?" I expect him to say "Australian terrier" like Killarney, since that was the breed we always had as children. Mackie was a stray Dad was asked to adopt, a detour on Dog Road.

He says, "I had a border collie when I was a teenager." He is looking off into the distance with a little smile of memory, which is good because it means he can't see my eyebrows fly up in the air. He adds, "A short-haired border collie. Black and white."

I don't know what a short-haired border collie

looks like. I've seen the fluffy ones. I didn't even know they came in another format.

As his birthday draws near I see a puppy advertised in the paper. I phone for more information. She is three months old, the straggler from a litter. That could be good – she'll have outgrown some of the earliest puppy hassles. She was born on a farm just outside Brisbane, and is one-quarter kelpie. A sturdy working dog.

I present the details to Dad. "What do you think? Would you like to see her?"

"Yes, I think I would." His smile is a little sheepish.

She is a gorgeous, galumphing pup, all big ears and impossibly long legs that seem to be made of rubber. She is shy and a little skittish. Her muzzle is white with a white blaze up the centre of her forehead and a black mask over both eyes. Her hair is short and silky.

Soon after, we are on the way home. Mum is in the passenger seat of my car, Dad is in the back, and alongside him on the floor is his wobbly puppy, his birthday present.

"Oh no! Pull over!"

Dad is out of the car faster than I've ever seen him move. Apparently the puppy was given a good breakfast this morning. And we can tell what it was, because it's now all over the floor. Fortunately she was sitting on newspaper in case of any puppy accidents.

A quick clean-up and I say, "Okay, let's get her home before she does it again."

"I'm not getting back in there."

"She's *your* pup. And it's only a bit of vomit. Don't be such a sook." It occurs to me how much a few years of pet ownership has changed me.

But Dad's expression is mutinous. And it's his birthday, after all.

We drive off with me in the back with the puppy, and Dad grinding the gears on my car because he's out of practice with a manual transmission. "I think you left my gearbox on the road back there. Whoa! Pull over!"

It seems the puppy hasn't had much practice travelling in cars, but I clean her up again and hold her high up on my lap so she can see out the window, just as I did for a smaller puppy a few years ago. "Home James, and don't spare the horses." The pup lurches and sways on my lap, eyes slowly rolling back in her head, and I could swear I can see a green tinge under her pure white muzzle.

We have one more "incident", and then finally we're home.

I ask Dad, "What will you call her?"

"I'd like her to have an Irish name. I was thinking of Bridget."

And so Bridget joins the family – Bridie for short.

❦

I TAKE KILLARNEY OVER TO MEET HER NEW… AUNT, IS it? Except that I don't like Bridie being labelled my sister, and so I prefer to think of the two dogs as cousins.

Killarney prefers to think of the new dog in her old territory as mincemeat. She rushes at Bridie, all guns blazing. Bridie is unimpressed and returns the favour. A brief skirmish ensues, and it's clear that the puppy can hold her own against big-headed terriers.

They settle down and learn to get along, although there's always a faint tension between them. It's not just Killarney. When Mum and Dad take Bridie to the dog park, she is aloof around other dogs. When they approach her to greet or to challenge, she simply veers away, making no eye contact and pursuing her own direction in life.

As Killarney and Bridie become more comfortable

around each other, they begin to rumble on a regular basis. This isn't mortal combat, just good clean fun. They run in big arcs and pounce on each other, rolling across the grass locked together, growling. Bridie is bigger than Killarney and growing fast and sometimes she lands heavily on my poor little terrier.

"I hope Killarney doesn't get injured doing this," I say with a frown.

"Oh, stop worrying," says Dad. "She's having fun. And it's good exercise for both of them."

Once Killarney has accepted another dog, she assumes they will curl up together. Bridie is reading from a different manual. When the weather turns cold, Killarney gets into Bridie's basket to snuggle with her. Bridie hops out of her basket and lies on the floor. Killarney walks over and lies on the floor close to Bridie. Bridie gets up and moves away. And the dance continues.

I arrive for a visit one day to find Mum taking clothes off the clothesline with a thunderous expression. Bridie is shut in Killarney's pen, skulking. "She tore the clothes off the line!"

I didn't see which educational principles were employed, but Bridie never does that again. She is scary smart, and she learns incredibly fast. She leaps around when excited so she has to learn to sit, especially when they're going into the shed to get her dinner. She sits after a fashion, but her tail is spring-loaded, and it's a very bouncy sit, with sporadic leaping eruptions during which she somehow keeps her bottom and most of her feet on the ground.

But education can only do so much. Another time I find Dad digging up their huge collection of bromeliads from the side garden. "She won't stop digging them up. We've tried everything. We're moving them out the front where she can't get at them."

"She eats the roots," Mum says. "Someone told me they cause hallucinations. Dogs get addicted to them."

I suggest that her full name should perhaps be Bridget Mayhem, and Bridie May for short. My suggestion is adopted unanimously.

At least she doesn't touch cane toads. In fact, she'd walk right on them in the yard at night and not even notice.

❧

MICHAEL ASKS ME TO PRESENT A NEW SEGMENT ON THE television program. This will mean being back on camera for the first time in well over a decade. I'm excited and a little nervous. This makes a change from the newsreading I did in my early twenties. Then I was utterly paralysed by nerves.

Sometimes I even fill in for Michael as the main presenter of the program. Wrangling a panel discussion with three guests in a "live to tape" environment is a whole new challenge for me, and I relish it.

CTA also indirectly helps me grow in other ways, by introducing me to authors who take part in the panel, some of whom want to self-publish. I've been using Adobe InDesign since it was Aldus PageMaker back in the eighties, but I never thought I'd get to design a book in it. In Sydney, there was a dedicated typesetter for that job. I love having the opportunity to do it myself.

I work with a group of psychologists, and while editing I learn much about how to manage my own stress. One says, "If you smile, your brain thinks you're happy." Killarney must have heard that, too.

☙❧

MUM AND DAD NEED TO GO AWAY FOR A FEW DAYS, AND Bridie is too young for their time-honoured practice of getting a neighbour to feed the dog. They bring her to me for petsitting. The tables have turned.

"She'd better not destroy my garden," I say. I'm

actually the world's worst and least motivated gardener, but I've been trying to grow a few vegetables in pots. So serious am I on this attempt that I've even bought myself a worm farm – a set of two big plastic tubs nested inside each other, with a lid. Scraps go in the top with the worms, worm castings drop through a grid into the bottom layer, and "worm juice" drips out a little tap on the front to collect in a plastic drink bottle I've placed there for the purpose. The worm juice is good for the plants too, and I add it to their water once a week.

I arrive home in the dark, wondering how the fur girls will have got on together through the day. They greet me at the back door, and they're both alive so that's a good first sign.

And then I see a dark splash on the concrete. In the dim light I can't tell what it is. Is it blood? Have they been fighting?! As I walk out I gasp. There are more slashes of dark colour here and there on the concrete and even up the walls, right up as far as the gate.

I grab Killarney and run my hands over her, feeling for wetness. I check my hands but they are clean. Then I do the same for Bridie, with the same result.

Mystified and a little panicky, I wander across the courtyard, looking for answers. I stumble on something underfoot. It is the worm juice bottle, shredded. In my head I see the vision of two dogs racing round my courtyard, growling and barking as worm juice flies left and right. I hope they didn't disturb the neighbours *too* much.

WHY NOT LOOK ON THE BRIGHT SIDE?

Joy is bigger when life is harder

MUM AND DAD ARE APPROACHING THEIR FIFTIETH wedding anniversary, and we're throwing them a party. Friends and family from around Australia and across the years are invited to a get together in the church hall. There will be music. There will be speeches. There will be a PowerPoint presentation with funny photos from the past.

There will be mini-quiches, hundreds of them.

And I'm cooking them.

Cooking skills aren't exactly at the top of my resume, but I'm not bad at mini-quiches. It's one of those "impossible" recipes, where you throw everything in together and it all comes out as a quiche.

It is eleven o'clock at night. I've got a lot of stress on at work, I've got a lot of mini-quiches to make, and I've got a raging head cold.

I can be sick next week. Tonight I've got a party to prepare for. As I chop up what looks to be half a side of bacon, Killarney hovers underfoot, ready to assist in any way possible.

I've broken a whole chookyard worth of eggs into my biggest mixing bowl, added cheese and milk and am about to add bacon when the bowl slips, skidding on the bench top. It tips over in slow motion as I shout "No-o-o-o!" Eggy mix pours gracefully onto the wool mat in front of my kitchen sink and spills over onto the tiles, forming an inland yellow sea.

I manage to grab the bowl before it's completely empty, and I consider my options. Crying is a strong favourite, but I've got too much to do and I really need to go to bed sooner than later. So the crying has to wait. I do a quick clean-up of the worst of the slip hazard on the tiles, look at the sodden mat and shrug, then turn to my bowl.

While I'm trying to guess how many ingredients need replacing, Killarney is doing her own mathematical equation. She slurps the eggs off the mat along a grid pattern, up one way, back the other. I glance at her and wonder how good it might be for her digestion – not just the quiche ingredients but the existing content of the mat. Let's just say it doesn't get vacuumed *incredibly* often. Oh well. By the time I'm putting the quiches in the oven twenty minutes later, she is still going. She is sucking on the pile now, not just licking it, and I can hear her sucking noises even over the oven fan.

҂ᴄ

THE PARTY AND THE QUICHES ARE A SUCCESS, KILLARNEY'S stomach recovers, and the following week I wake up one morning so sick I can't lift my head from the pillow.

Somewhere along the way I've become my mother and I can't possibly miss a day of work, so I try to struggle out of bed. Besides, how will CTA get the television program to air without me?

But somehow, they have to. I can barely walk as far as the bathroom. I feed Killarney, then just go back to bed. My whole body is on fire, every muscle and joint in agony. Is it the reward for saying "I can be sick next week"? When the illness drags on for weeks, tests are inconclusive but my doctor thinks it is Ross River Fever – a severe mosquito-borne virus that usually lasts about six weeks, and can then turn chronic in some people.

I'm on a countdown to attending the Frankfurt Book Fair in Germany – the biggest meeting of publishing people in the world. Ten convention halls, many of them multi-floor, and a quarter of a million publishing people in one place. It's the pilgrimage of a lifetime for a bookish person, and everything is paid. I can't possibly not go.

Somehow, with a cornucopia of supplements from a naturopath and a program of serious prayer from my friends and family, I make it to Frankfurt. Somehow, I walk around those ten halls, and I meet a lot of people and do a lot of things.

Back in Brisbane, I stop taking the supplements and fall in a heap again. It looks like I'm one of the chosen percentage who get the chronic version. Month follows month and my life is still full of pain and exhaustion. Having a naturally peppy dog who is devoid of empathy can be tough when you feel like a limp rag every day of your life. But it can also give you a reason to get out of bed and soldier on.

☙

THERE'S MORE THAN ONE CRAZY ANIMAL IN MY HOUSE, as evidenced by the fact that my chosen form of recuperation from a crippling post-viral syndrome is to make a booking to hike New Zealand's Milford Track. It's 53.5 km (33.25 miles) through the most dramatic mountains I have ever seen, the mountains other mountains want to be when they grow up. It is cut off from the world – no roads, no mobile phone signal.

And even when I'm well, I'm no athlete. I mostly like hiking for the photography and the snacks.

But I've heard that consistent exercise can help some people with post-viral fatigue. I'll need powerful motivation to exercise when I'm in this much pain. Fear of requiring a rescue helicopter on the side of a remote New Zealand fiord is powerful motivation.

For years, I've been yearning to hike the Milford Track, as a research expedition for the mystery/thriller novel I've been longing to write. It's about a group of old friends with past secrets who go hiking in Fiordland and don't all come home. I got the idea during a holiday around New Zealand in the mid-nineties and it's been festering ever since, waiting for me to have time to write it – waiting for someone to give me "permission" to write it. It's been one page long for a decade. The journalist in me needs some facts from which to springboard the story. I need to interview people. I need to walk up and down those incredible mountains so I know what it feels like.

But none of my hiking friends has ever been available at a time when I can do the trek. I've dreamed about it, and dithered, and wondered. It's not safe to hike alone, and I'd be too scared to do that anyway. But now, under the onslaught of viral attack, I bite the bullet and book in for the expensive guided version of the walk, the one with hot meals and hot showers.

Killarney watches, curious, as I lace up my hiking boots and load sacks of flour and sugar into my rucksack in preparation for a training hike in suburbia. "You can't come, Puddly. I'll barely survive this even *without* trying to drag you away from all the big dogs in the street."

Short training hikes gradually lengthen. Every few days I add another sack of flour to the rucksack. I'm in agony after every training session, but each time I can do a little more for the same amount of pain.

I borrow a stepping machine and put it in my lounge room where I can climb imaginary hills in front of the television. I can only do two minutes at first, but I gradually increase it.

I also establish a training circuit up in the hills, on the roads around Mum and Dad's shed. They volunteer to get up early on Saturday mornings to be my support team, preparing meals and snacks for my pit stops and providing moral support. Ever the careful one, Dad hands me two fluoro orange flags. "Here, stick these into the back of your rucksack, so drivers can see you." I feel pretty stupid with them there, but I do it, because, well, he's my Dad.

Killarney lollops around on the grass with my parents while I set off down the road, concentrating on putting one foot in front of another, trying to keep my breathing rhythmic and my pace consistent.

When the weather gets unseasonably hot and I need to start training at five am, we head up the night before to sleep in the shed. I find a snakeskin, shed by its wearer not all that long ago by the looks of it.

"Can Killarney be inside with us please?"

"She'll be fine," Dad says. "None of our dogs have ever had a problem here."

"I won't get any sleep if I'm worrying about her."

He sighs and shakes his head. We settle for the night with Killarney in her basket leashed to the table leg so she can't roam around.

I wake in pitch darkness and sit bolt upright. There are no street lights here. I'm not even sure what woke me. I fumble for my torch, flick it on and direct it to Killarney's basket. She isn't in it. She is at the full reach of her taut leash, ears forward, staring fixedly at a snake oozling its way along the base of the wall.

I'm out of my bed like it's spring-loaded. "Snake!"

While my parents are still thinking about waking up, I'm circling round behind Killarney and getting a grip on her leash so I can drag her away from the danger as steadily and quietly as I can.

I can't be sure of snake identification by torch-light, especially not without seeing its belly, but the telltale gleam of the coppery-bronze of the eastern brown is enough for me to be very, very cautious. It continues along the base of the wall, and then I watch it slither straight up the vertical steel column before disappearing onto the roof beam. So much for "brown snakes can't climb".

"I'm not staying in here."

Mum concurs. She and I pack up the dog and a blanket each, and settle as best we can on the bench seats of my parents' Kombi microbus. Killarney is on the floor between us, fidgeting and fuffing. It's going to be a long night.

Dad shakes his head and climbs back into bed to sleep soundly till morning.

❧

A LITTLE OVER A YEAR AFTER THE MOSQUITO BITE THAT made me sick, I'm standing at the beginning of the Milford Track, smiling widely to conceal my terror. The boat has just left and my only way out from here is my legs or a rescue mission.

Killarney is back in Brisbane in the care of the built-in petsitters. I like to think she misses me. I'm kidding myself, since she's a social butterfly who has never pined a day in her life, but I like to think it.

The mountains are everything I've dreamed of. They are also my worst nightmare. The uphill is heavy going with some intimidating drops off to the side, but I can cope if I keep stopping to rest. I'm strong with the pack uphill – all that training has made a world of difference. The view at the top of Mackinnon Pass is so beautiful I swear I can hear angels singing.

The descent that follows, however, is beyond a joke. Four hours of boulder-hopping down a perilously steep slope, sometimes out in the open, sometimes through rainforest and waterfalls. It's hard to know how I could have prepared any more effectively for a four-hour downhill that constantly chops and changes, angling ankles, feet and knees – twisting and turning, grabbing and slipping, all while controlling the weight of a twelve kilogram pack. How could anyone train for that except by doing it? After a couple of hours my legs are so wobbly I can barely control their direction, and I still have a couple of hours to go. The guide walking behind me can see my form, and offers again and again to take my pack, even though she's tiny and already carrying a huge pack.

She tells me about a time two female guides had to carry someone down that mountain for two hours. "I'd rather carry your pack than you."

"I really want to do it myself." We keep going.

After what feels like a hundred years of struggle she says, "Shh, listen!" Even over my own noisy breathing, I can hear a gentle humming. "Know what that is? That's the generator at Quintin Lodge!"

I couldn't have imagined a day when I would feel so glad to hear a generator in a pristine wilderness. I hobble into the lodge and I can't stop grinning. I did it. Somehow. On my own legs.

Several others have taken a tumble during the afternoon, and there's a sense of camaraderie among the walkers that wasn't there before. A bond formed through surviving something hard. One hiker is playing sing-along songs at the piano – something he's done every night of the trek – but this time even a very elegant group of women from Melbourne are joining in.

The fourth and final day is easy by comparison, even though my knees are bone-on-bone and very swollen. I walk with a sweet and shy Japanese couple who don't have much English. She is limping. What a trial by fire their honeymoon is turning out to be.

At our morning tea stop she says, with huge eyes, "So tired already."

I nod vigorously. "Me too."

A few miles later as I step down off a rock and let out an involuntary groan, she says, "Me too!" and we both have to stop walking till we've finished giggling. Apparently, both pain and humour cross most language barriers. Her new husband waits patiently in the background.

Each time we pass another mile marker, my new friend and I raise our arms in the air and cheer, shouting the number. We're running out of time to catch the last ferry back to civilisation, so for the last couple of miles I pick up speed, using my hiking poles to propel myself forward. Endorphins kick in and my pain ebbs away.

Finally, we have our photo taken standing together under the marker that declares the end of the

Milford Track. We are both grinning so widely our faces may well split in half. Lots of other walkers have reached the end much faster than we have. They are athletes, ticking another famous hike off their list. But I challenge any of them to match our joy.

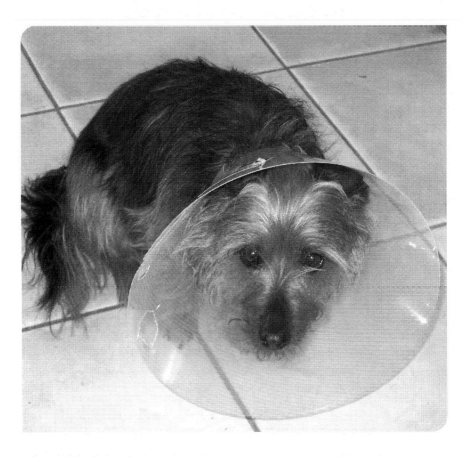

ENDURING THE CONE OF SHAME.

LESSON 12:
Joy survives in the worst of times

AFTER THE TREK, I SPEND TEN DAYS IN THE TINY TOWN of Te Anau, doing interviews and library research. I hobble around town on my ruined knees, and take hundreds more photos. I charter a light plane with two strangers, and fly over the Fiordland mountains and the real Poison Bay, gripping the door handle for dear life as updraft after updraft buffets the tiny aircraft. The manuscript for *Poison Bay* expands to 11,000 words, but then grinds to a halt when I get a call to say Dad is in hospital. He's had a minor stroke. The novel loses its place in my head altogether a few weeks later when he is scheduled for an urgent heart bypass operation just before Christmas.

Serious complications mean the strange twilight half-life of the Intensive Care Unit becomes home for Mum and me for long hours on endless days. Our church mobilises squadrons of people to pray for him and for us. The doctors make no promises.

All we can do is wait to see if my darling Dad will live or die or be in a coma forever.

I have to tackle my phobia about hospitals head-on. My father needs me. My mother needs me.

My experience as a baby journalist twenty years earlier comes in handy. I didn't know what to ask or where to stand, but I developed a calm, professional face to mask the nerves. Now I'm working at looking calm, speaking in a measured way, breathing deeply – while a cyclone rages in my head. The funny thing though is that the act of trying to appear calm seems to be helping control my own terror too. One of the psychologists I do editing work for calls that "fake it till you can make it".

When I'm home alone, then I can let the pressure out in tears. Holding Killarney while I do it is excellent therapy. She is thrilled to see me each time, and my tears don't seem to trouble her.

 intlfi

THE DAY DAD WIGGLES HIS TOES ON COMMAND MAKES our hearts sing. It means he is still in there somewhere. When he finally is fully conscious, he has a long road ahead – but what a joy to talk to him and hear him answer!

We are humble and thankful, because we know

so many others in our situation do not get a miracle. Dad is in hospital for six long weeks, and he gets to know the menu rotation off by heart. When he finally comes home on a summer day hot enough to boil your blood, he is weak as a kitten. The power goes out, meaning we have no air-conditioning. And if we ever needed air-con in their house, it's today. I chase electricians and try to keep everyone calm, even though I'd quite like to fall apart myself.

It's months before he can digest food properly or walk with confidence. But gradually he comes back into his life. Initially we have to keep both Killarney and Bridie away from the long surgical wounds where they removed blood vessels to use in his heart, because of the lingering infection risk. But in time, he is throwing toys for Bridie and scruffling his granddog's blonde head again.

I'm challenged by all I've seen and experienced. The long hours at hospital bedsides have tilted my thinking. Perhaps it's time to be practical. I've been doing a lot of satisfying work for interesting clients, but so many of them are charities or Christian organisations who pay very little. It's one thing to be content with a modest income; it's another to realise you are never going to pay off your home loan in your lifetime.

I approach one of my clients with a proposal, and within weeks I am working almost full-time for them, in a marketing and communications role. My business is squeezed into one day a fortnight. I can still do the odd writing or editing job in my spare time, but they will be minimal. I learn something about freelancing though, when the company charges a client for my work at $115 an hour. They only pay me a fraction of that. It finally dawns on me that it's so high because it has to cover the whole cost of providing my services – the IT workers, the accountants, the building, the computer and desk. I have been charging clients a wage rate, not a service fee. My fee should have been covering all my expenses, plus the time I had to spend on business activities that were not my money-earning work. If only I'd learned this a lot sooner, I might still be freelancing.

My novel is put to one side. There is no time for such trivialities in the seriousness of daily life.

❦

KILLARNEY IS EIGHT YEARS OLD WHEN I FIND ANOTHER lump, up near her "armpit". With all that's been going on with Dad, I haven't had the mental wherewithal to take her to the vet and get it checked, or even to worry about it – although I do worry a little about not worrying about it. Finally, in October we make it to the vet, and I really don't like the feel of the lump. It's more diffuse than the earlier ones, less discrete.

"We'd better take it out," says Tom. He finds another smaller lump further around on her ribs, and he's going to take that out too. The surgery is scheduled for Wednesday morning, and as usual that means a bath on Tuesday night, and no food or water after midnight. I'm a veterinary veteran; I know the drill.

She comes home Wednesday evening after her surgery so she'll feel safe in her own home, and I make up a special bed of towels on the floor so she can lie out flat and not have to twist her wounds. Her belly and side have been shaved and are blue with whatever antiseptic they paint them with during surgery. My sister and her family are over for a birthday dinner and they each stop to give her pats as they walk past her limp form while she sleeps off the anaesthetic.

Now and then she gets up and tries to move around on wobbly legs, groaning with the effort. It breaks my heart to have to watch my unstoppable dog in this state, but it's part of my job. So I look positive and take tender care of her.

Saturday I notice that she's pulled a couple of stitches out, so we're back at the vet. Restitching is an infection risk, so we just have to wait for it to mend itself. But we can't risk any more unauthorised suture removal, so she has to have an Elizabethan collar – the plastic-flower pot on the head, the Cone of Shame.

She hates it and sits hunched over, peering at me with a look of woe from under her big plastic helmet. She runs into furniture because she can't judge her own width, and then she gets cross.

The next Wednesday rolls around and I find another lump the size of a marble that came up virtually overnight. I get an emergency appointment at the vet, and it turns out the pathology results are back, too. The tumour removed was cancer, the malignant invasive kind, red of tooth and claw.

"We need to check her for any more lumps," says Tom. He frowns at the one I've discovered on her neck, and finds another somewhere else. "We'll need to remove them."

"When?"

"Tomorrow."

I gasp. She hasn't even had the first round of

stitches removed yet. I'm trying to hold my face in a neutral position but Tom and Hayley give me compassionate looks and I dissolve.

I'm back after Thursday's Round Two to collect a dog who is now half-bald and has a total of five surgical wounds on different parts of her body. Tom found yet another one when she was on the table.

"It went well," says Tom. And then he grins. "The one on her shoulder was her microchip. We tested it and it still works, so we put it back in."

The new wound on the front of her neck rules out a collar, and therefore an Elizabethan collar.

"How will I stop her removing the new stitches?"

"You could try putting socks on her back legs," says Hayley. "That won't stop her scratching, but at least it can prevent her getting her claws into the sutures."

Once Killarney is sufficiently awake from her second general anaesthetic in a week, she is wearing a pair of long blue socks on her hind legs, tied together above her tail. I can't help giggling just a little under my breath and she gives me a reproachful look.

Saturday comes around and it's time for Killarney's first set of stitches to be removed. I can't get a leash on her due to her neck wound. Eventually,

I wrap her in a big, blue-and-white fluffy towel and lift her carefully.

She gives me a beseeching look as I put her gently on the floor of the car, but I speak in positive tones and only cry on the inside.

As we approach the vet's office, Killarney – ensconced in a towel with only her head sticking out – starts barking like mad. A big bull terrier coming the other way takes it personally and starts bellowing ferociously.

His owner wrangles him while I dash past into the waiting room with my loud, wriggling bundle of fear and pain. I head straight for an empty corner and stand there as Killarney's bark becomes a full-throated yollop-yollop-yollop. The bull terrier out on the footpath begins to howl. A woman waiting in another corner with a tiny quivering puppy glares at me in shocked disapproval. I turn away and close my eyes as Killarney continues to yelp at the full extent of her lungpower.

Hayley slips out from the examination room and there's no prizes for guessing how she knew we'd arrived. "Come through here, Belinda." I think she's probably slipping me in out of order, and I'm desperately grateful.

The stitches are out quickly and we're out of

there. On the way home I stop at an unfamiliar butcher shop to get Killarney some fresh beef to try to cheer her up.

"How's your morning been?" the young butcher says with a cheery smile.

I accidentally tell the truth. "Actually, I've just been to the vet with my dog."

He pauses mid-meat, frowning. "What's wrong with your dog?"

"She's had surgery. The beef is for her." Then, suddenly thinking of all the starving people in the world and the fact I'm in a low-income suburb I add, "She doesn't normally get that sort of thing."

He nods, and his eyes are kind. "You want to give her a treat." He's swift on the scales. I suspect he's trying to hide that he's giving me more than I've asked for. "I hope your dog gets better." I walk out of the shop with my spirits lifted. He is out of pocket by 69c and a couple of kind words, but it is a priceless boost to my awful day.

The second set of pathology results from the vet comes in a few days later and they're good. One lump is non-invasive, the other is benign.

"What do we do next?"

"Just keep an eye on her," says Tom. "If you find another lump, bring her in."

"Is that all? Even though she's had such a bad tumour?"

"It was small." I can almost see a shrug down the phone line. "We had a dog with recurring mammary cancer who lived to be fifteen."

Tom's not scared. I'll have to figure out how to do that.

∽

I'M INSPIRED. MY PARENTS HAVE BUILT A NEW BACK VE-randa on their house and enclosed it with security mesh that looks similar to flyscreen, but is much stronger and even burglar proof.

"What if I turned the pergola into an outdoor room?"

Dad nods. "You'd get a lot more use out of it." Snake Central is also Mosquito Central, so I'm rarely outside after dark.

While I'm phoning builders and getting quotes, Mum and Dad report that they've seen just the thing for me on a television show featuring new Australian inventions. It's called a Pet Loo and is designed for apartment dwellers – a sturdy plastic device topped by a special kind of artificial grass that is supposed to repel odours.

If I could get one of those for Killarney and

snake-proof my outdoor room, how much easier might life be? She could be safe, and yet comfortable. Could I even get to the point where I didn't have to come home every night steeling myself for the potential sight of a snakebitten dog?

The builder thinks I'm nuts, but I don't care. The walls must extend right down to the concrete, since the customary drainage gap would just be a snake superhighway at my house. I'll have to clean it out some other way. And I want silicon sealant around all the gaps.

Once the builder hands over the keys and leaves, I do another round with the silicon sealant, making sure to plug every gap that could imaginably admit a sneaky, body-flattening Houdini-snake. It's amazing what a home handyman I've become for the sake of this dog.

My parents view the new room with interest and satisfaction. "Well Killarney," says Dad with a smile, "what do you think of your palace?" The name sticks.

The full suffocating heat of summer arrives, and I'm sitting in the palace sipping a cold drink when Killarney alerts. She is over at the steel mesh, starting intently, ears forward. On the ground outside, a large eastern brown snake is swaying, looking at her, head raised in the characteristic S shape they adopt when preparing to strike.

What if it strikes and hits the mesh and some of the venom is squeezed out of its fangs and it flies through and lands on her and can you absorb it through your SKIN?!

Killarney is so still she could be carved from stone. The snake blinks first and lowers its head, oozling off around the side of the palace. I breathe a sigh of relief. There are no guarantees that my outdoor room is completely snake-proof, but I think snake-anxiety might be a smaller part of my life in days to come.

❧

LIFE CONTINUES TO UNDULATE. KILLARNEY GOES TO THE built-in petsitters for a couple of weeks while I hike around the natural beauties of Tasmania with a friend. Killarney comes with me when I travel north for my niece's eighteenth birthday. She's a good traveller who sits happily in the car for hours, and my sister's family love her.

A few weeks later, my darling mother has a severe illness and we end up back at the Intensive Care Unit. The specialist recognises us and says, "Ah, yes. Frequent Fliers."

I try to help Mum and advocate for her while giving my dad as much support as I can. On the inside, I'm terrified and would rather fall in a heap. Dad and I pause as we're trudging up the long hill to the hospital, yet again. He is dizzy because his funny heartbeat has started again, thanks no doubt to the strain of being unable to "rescue" the woman he loves from this drama. Seeing her sick is agony for him.

"We've got plenty of time," I say. "Just lean on this fence for a minute."

Dad catches his breath and says to me with moist eyes, "You're my rock." These words are indescribably precious to me. I hate hospitals and illness, I dread losing one of my parents, and each day of this is a nightmare for me. But if I really am helping him through it then my own pain is worth it.

Mum recovers, although it's a long road for her too.

☙

I'M IN MY EARLY FORTIES AND THE BIOLOGICAL CLOCK IS about to detonate. My seventy-something mother says, "Why don't you try the internet? That girl from church met her husband on the internet, and he's very nice." So I try online dating for a while.

Obviously, any serious candidate is going to have to be a dog lover to cope with my crazy pet. I have coffee with a bunch of nice men, but there are no fireworks. I'm disappointed, and yet glad that I've given it a shot. There'll probably be no children for me now, but at least I won't have to look back and say, "I wish I'd tried harder."

I shoot for – and get – a new job. This one is also in the corporate world. It's full-time. My publishing business is squeezed into a tiny corner of my life. My novel is forgotten.

As Mum becomes more like herself, she and Dad start travelling again. They seem a little unsure about the vast distances of the Australian outback, now that they've discovered that it can be good to have medical assistance close by. They travel shorter distances, or stay near the heavily populated coastline.

One evening they call me from the road, and it's clear the old instincts have not been completely erased. They've taken a back route, got away from the highway.

"I'll have to be quick," says Mum. "The mobile phone battery is about to die. We're staying in a caravan park behind an old pub. There's no one else here except a man who lives here permanently in his caravan."

Who lives permanently in a caravan behind a remote pub? Norman Bates? "Well look after yourselves. Make sure you lock the doors on the van."

"Oh, we'll be all right. Bridie won't let anyone near us."

I'm relieved when they get home safely. With all life's ins and outs, the home front is so much less complicated now that Killarney is separated from her serpentine friends. She is happy and healthy, and a blessing to come home to as the world shifts and changes around me.

"I'M HERE FOR YOU."

LESSON 13:
Joy is surrendering control

KILLARNEY IS TEN YEARS OLD WHEN MY DAD DIES. He is there, and then he isn't.

It is a brain haemorrhage, caused by the cocktail of blood thinners the doctors put him on for his heart. He visits four doctors for different reasons in the three days after he hits his head, but not one of them notices he is dying.

A chasm opens up in my universe, and I don't know how to look into it. I cuddle Killarney for comfort, and wonder if she can sense anything from me, although as usual she never looks sad. She can't possibly understand that her Grandad is never going to scruffle her hair again. I can't understand it myself.

I stay at Mum's place so we can keep each other company through the first endless, sleepless, echoing night. The next evening we need a trip to the shops, because family are coming and we're out of milk. Even at the end of the world, you still need milk.

We stop at a friend's place on the way. We are greeted by a noisy white terrier, and I pause for a little more dog psychology. The animal has the kind of fur that will send me into sneezes and itches, but I don't care. I'll just wash the allergens off my hands before we leave.

I've had the dog all up my arms, so I take my watch off and rest it on the edge of the handbasin, and give my hands and forearms a good wash. "Are you scrubbing for surgery?" That's what my Dad would have said.

It's getting late as we pull up in the supermarket car park, thick-headed from grief and exhaustion. I quickly check the time to see if the shops are still open. My wrist is bare. "Oh no. My watch. I must have left it at your friend's place."

We muddle through a plan for me to go back for the watch, while Mum proceeds into the supermarket before it closes.

Back at the friend's place, I stand on the doorstep and awkwardly explain. She is all warmth and helpfulness. "Oh come in and we'll find it!"

Together, we search the bathroom. Not there. The hallway and loungeroom. Not there. In the dark I start to examine the front lawn between house and car. Not there.

Embarrassed, I head back to the supermarket. I'm hunting around the gravel of the car park when Mum appears. She is leaning on a shopping trolley almost as though it's a walking frame.

"I didn't find the watch," I explain. "I thought it could be on the ground here, but it's too dark to see."

"We might have to come back in the morning and see if we can find it."

"I guess so." It wasn't an expensive watch, but it hurts to lose something else. My eyes scan down to Mum's trolley. It is entirely empty. My eyebrows shoot up. "Where's the milk?"

Mum looks down and we freeze in a tableau, four eyebrows elevated, two brains vacant. Mum is first to think of an answer. "I must have left it at the checkout."

Fortunately, the checkout operator had enough sense to put the milk aside. Back at Mum's house, I sit on the bed in the spare room trying to sort myself out for another night away from home. I shove my sleeves up my arms, and automatically check the time. 9.30 pm. I stare open-mouthed at the dial gleaming back at me from my wrist. My right wrist, not the left one. And I start giggling.

Mum walks to the doorway and stares at me. "What are you laughing at?"

"Look!" I point at the watch. I can hardly draw breath, let alone speak. "It was on the wrong wrist!"

"Oh!" She starts to giggle too. The immense pressure of the past twenty-four hours releases itself like a dam-burst. Inane laughter wells up in us both, surrounding and overwhelming us. We giggle and snort until we get the hiccups, and tears run down our faces. And then we start crying. And then we hug each other again.

❧

THERE ARE A LOT MORE TEARS AND HUGS IN THE MONTHS that follow. I hold myself together all day at work and during the train ride, and then once I'm in my car, the tears start, bursting out of my soul like a force of nature. I howl and sob in the privacy of that ten-minute journey, then stop when I drive into the village. I have a shower and put on Dad's scratchy red wool dressing gown, the one he wore during our last conversation. Mum had washed it and saw me looking at it, and she said, "Would you like it?" and

I said "Yes. I would." Each time I put it on it's like a hug from him.

My housekeeping, always quixotic, becomes non-existent. Dishes and papers pile up and I just can't seem to clean up the mess. There's something in me that recoils from it, and I think it must be something to do with the grief process. Even when I have a spare hour, I don't want to use it to clean, I just want to sit in a heap.

I go to Mum's place often for dinner now, and I sit in Dad's seat so that it won't be empty. Bridie seems confused. How can we tell her where he's gone? I abandon my own church and start going to church with Mum – the one she attended with Dad – otherwise she might not leave the house on Sundays. Thankfully, she is still teaching her exercise classes, and they give some structure to her week. My sofa-bed gets a lot of use and so does Mum's spare room. We keep each other company as much as we can. I phone her in the morning to check she's going okay. We pray for each other over the phone at bedtime, and it's enormously comforting.

૯৲૩

I'VE BEEN TERRIFIED THESE PAST FEW YEARS BY THE thought of losing one of my parents. Scientists talk about an Extinction Level Event (ELE), such as a comet hitting the earth and destroying all life. Well, loss of a parent felt like an ELE to me, when it was still in the future. Maybe it was worse because I had no separate family of my own, I don't know. But I've worked so hard to fend it off and keep them safe.

Now, the worst thing I could ever imagine has happened. And I'm still breathing. It wasn't an ELE, after all. Fear does not always tell the truth.

All my attempts at control – getting Dad to hospital when he was ill, or trying to stop him from climbing trees or taking risks – they only gave me an illusion of control. When it was his time, it was his time, and there was nothing I could do about it. Someone else was taking charge of that.

But just as I had less control than I thought over his death, his death had less control than I thought it would have over me. I miss him so much it's like a physical agony, but somehow I will survive even this. As week follows week and I try to engage in life as best I can, I can feel in my bones that one day I will even be happy again.

ɘ

THREE MONTHS AFTER MY DAD DIED, I FIND MYSELF IN hospital. I don't know how to be the one in the bed. I'm the one who sits beside the bed, helping, advocating, offering comfort.

"It's pancreatitis," they say. "We'll do tests in the morning."

I know they are looking for cancer. I sit up in my lonely hospital bed in the night and all I can think is, "What will happen to Mum if I die too?"

The results come back: it doesn't seem to be cancer. "We think it's probably your gallbladder. A blockage can cause pancreatitis."

As I leave hospital five days later, Mum goes in. Her trouble? Gallbladder. Quick work by a surgeon saves her life. I struggle to be any help to her.

As Mum recovers, I go back into hospital. Now we'll be able to tell stories at parties about our two-for-one gallbladder operations. I emerge from the anaesthetic into a psychotropic medication reaction that induces five hours of terror. The hospital staff close the curtains around my bed and leave me to deal with it alone.

We both struggle to pick up. I've lost nearly a quarter of my bodyweight. I subsist on banana sandwiches and crackers with tuna, because I can digest them. The panic attacks I experienced in my twenties and thought I'd grown out of return with a vengeance. So does the irritable bowel. I spend far too much time in the ladies room, praying desperately for peace.

❦

THROUGH ALL OF THIS, KILLARNEY IS AS POSITIVE AS ever. Need her to sleep in a different place? No problem. Need her to wait at home for hours while I'm at work or at Mum's? She'll be quiet and content with her toys while I'm out, and do a happy dance when I come home. Need a therapeutic cuddle from her while I weep? You bet.

I throw soft toys in the house for her, again and again. This is good fun, but hide and seek becomes her favourite game. I sneak away when she's not looking and crouch down behind a piece of furniture. I listen to the click-click-pause of her claws on the tiles as she goes from room to room, looking for me. When she finally tracks me down I giggle and she leaps with joy and runs in circles barking her head off. She *knows* it's a game, and she loves that I'll make a fool of myself with her. It's one of my rare moments of laughter during those months.

Just before Christmas, I find another lump on her. It's removed and turns out to be benign, but the following morning I discover that she has pulled out every single one of her stitches. "She's very good at suture removal," says Tom, inspecting the wound. "Very neat." He doesn't want to re-stitch. It's an infection risk.

The wound gradually closes and she powers through life undaunted as ever. "Puddleduck, if you could just wait ten days and *then* take your stitches out, we'd have a perfect system."

ALASKAN SLED DOGS: SO MUCH
MORE THAN I IMAGINED.

LESSON 14:
Joy isn't where most people think I should look

IN THE STIFLING HEAT OF JANUARY I BOOK TO GO ON A cruise to Alaska with Mum for September. To me, a cruise sounds like a big floating bingo hall, full of people drinking and eating too much, all trapped in each other's company as the ocean rages around them. I love the sea, but I'm more about looking at it or swimming in it than being on it. I grew up in a sailing family and was dogged by seasickness, forever "feeding the fish" over the side. But I've grown out of that now. An Alaskan cruise is something Mum talked about doing with Dad, and they never got around to it. Dad loved the ocean, and boats of any kind. He wanted to see Alaska, another frontier like the Australian outback he adored, albeit with slightly different weather!

I like the idea that Mum and I can be travel buddies, because I've travelled alone so much. It's an upside to the awful absence of my father. I get relief from energy-sapping humidity at home by thinking about glaciers and looking up the weather forecast for Juneau. Plus I'm delighted to find that a seven-day cruise is much cheaper than I anticipated. Sometimes Mum doesn't seem very strong, and I wonder if we'll even get to Alaska. I bat the thought away.

I am a fiercely independent traveller. For years, I've made all my travel bookings via the internet with my Lonely Planet travel guide at my side. This time I opt to be passive and let a travel agent handle all the arrangements. We'll add some time in the Canadian Rockies, while we're there. We will go in a group on a bus, and be herded around like sheep, because it means that if Mum suffers a health event, there'll be locals on hand to guide us to assistance.

&

For a while now I've been reading the hymnbook at church by peering *under* my glasses, but that doesn't mean anything is wrong with my eyes. The optometrist disagrees, and I leave his office with a prescription for multi-focal glasses. I am so old that I now need old-people glasses.

I complain about it to Lauren. "I'm falling apart. When did this happen?"

"I only look in the mirror if I have to," she says.

"Oh well. Swine flu will probably carry us off before we get *too* old." The news is full of swine flu hysteria. "Did you notice that the Australian government delegation that was caught in Mexico was led by Senator Hogg?"

"I went to primary school with a couple of Hoggs."

"Does that predispose you to swine flu? Or confer immunity?"

"And whatever happened to SARS?"

My Japanese friend Misaki is flying in tomorrow. She got a good deal on a flight to the Gold Coast, a regional airport located a three-hour public transport nightmare away from my house. "She's afraid she won't find the right shuttle bus," I tell Lauren. "She's used to Osaka Kansai airport, which is the size of a small planet and has automated trains that speak in disembodied voices. I've tried to explain Gold Coast airport won't be so big. It's basically a big tin shed with a van out the front, isn't it?"

"Probably."

"It'll be nice to see her." Misaki shares my faith and has emailed me about her eagerness to pray together.

"It would be hard to be a Christian in Japan. It'll

be good for her to have you to encourage her for a while."

And for me to have her encouragement, too. Misaki will stay at Mum's place, because I'm at work such long hours. I'm hoping it will lift the spirits of both. Misaki is such a polite and positive person she's a joy to have around.

Mum calls the next day to let me know she has successfully collected my friend from the train station, and the journey went well. She puts Misaki on the line.

"Thank you for everything Berinda. I worry too much."

You and me both, sister. But the weekend spent together gives us all a lift. Her visit gives Mum and I the excuse to do special things we haven't done in ages, like drive up to a restaurant in the mountains and eat a special meal.

When it's time for her to fly out again all too soon, we three drive down to the Gold Coast together, making an overnight holiday of it. We walk on the beach at dusk and the wind blows our hair into crazy styles. We find a really good meal at a pub for a scandalously low price.

The motel near the airport that I found on the internet is basic but nice. However, just as I fall asleep at ten pm, a gang of children start playing a very loud game of hide-n-seek-n-shriek over the back fence. I lie in bed thinking of suitable old-bat things to shout at their parents. Mum and Misaki sleep blissfully on.

In the morning, we take Misaki to the airport, where I spot several people wearing surgical masks to protect themselves from swine flu. I look at Mum and hope she hasn't picked up any germs. We don't need that after everything else that's gone on in our lives. But I shrug it off and keep moving.

ℭℌ

AT ELEVEN YEARS OLD, KILLARNEY STARTS TO HAVE tummy troubles. The usual flea treatments seem to be causing her internal chaos so I have to stop them, and chemicals around the house are altogether a bad idea.

One evening she is in so much pain that I take her to the vet the next day. I'm afraid that he's going to tell me her innards are riddled with cancer, spread from the mammary tumour I didn't deal with fast enough a couple of years ago.

But instead Tom says, "It looks like pancreatitis to me."

"Really?" I make a lame joke about how it must

run in families, but on the inside I'm reeling. It has taken me many months to get over the fear of another wildcat episode of pancreatitis for myself.

He says, "Lots of older dogs get it. One fatty meal can be enough to trigger an episode."

"I gave her the skin off a barbecue chicken the other day."

"Yep, that would be it."

Killarney recovers, but more stomach trouble ensues. Some of it is serious enough that she has to be hooked up to a drip for three days. My home toolkit now includes an electrolyte drink for pets and a healing antibiotic medicine. I get to know the instructions for it off by heart.

The vet also sends me home with a special dry food with a wince-worthy price tag. "Cook her some homemade food. Steer clear of fat – it has to be very lean. And don't give her beef or chicken. She's probably developed an intolerance to them. Try lamb."

Yeah, lamb. One of my favourite meats, and yet one I don't eat very often because it's so expensive. And a meat that is naturally very fatty. The neglected filleting knife I got in a set a few years earlier finds its purpose as I spend hours each week slicing every sliver of fat out of marbled cuts of lamb. My dog dines on choice cuts while I chisel frozen crusts of bread out of the back of the freezer for my own meals. I tell myself that her food is expensive, but not nearly as expensive as three days at the vet on a drip.

Lauren is the only friend I can really talk to about all this nonsense. We are both in full-time elderpet digestion maintenance. She has a new anti-depressant for Cocoa the crazy-cat.

"The vet has recommended a chicken flavour," she says. "Maybe I should try some."

"If it's any good, get a bottle for me too." I'm kidding of course, but it would be nice not to worry so much.

დ

THE MEDIA IS HAVING A FIELD DAY WITH SWINE FLU. AND then I read about a cruise ship being told not to dock in north Queensland because three crewmembers had swine flu. I'll be on a cruise ship soon.

I wish someone would hold the media accountable for the distress they cause anxious people by exaggerating danger for the sake of entertainment. And then I think back to some of the beat-ups I wrote myself back in my journalism days when we needed to find a lead story on a slow news day. If we'd had the same continuous coverage technologies back then, would I have joined in?

☙

IT'S THE YEAR OF TRYING TO PUT SOME JOY BACK INTO our lives, so I decide to take Mum whale watching on Moreton Bay. She's wanted to do it for ages. And it will be a good opportunity to test how her stomach copes with being at sea, since we'll be stuck out there for a whole seven days soon enough.

Mum has a lovely time. But once they stop and idle the engines so we can watch a whale in the distance, and the boat starts slopping about in the ocean swells, it's the end of me. I try looking at the horizon, shutting my eyes, eating a dry bread roll, but nothing works. I end up lying on my back on a hard, narrow little bench with my eyes shut, clutching a paper bag. If Migaloo the white whale came right alongside wearing a pink bonnet and sang the whole Hallelujah Chorus, I would *not* sit up.

By the time we've been back on sheltered water ten minutes, the nausea evaporates as suddenly as it came.

Mum is disappointed the whales weren't closer. She says, "I think I'd like to go again in a smaller boat."

"Well you enjoy yourself, I'm not coming."

ᑕᒎ

IT'S TIME TO LEAVE FOR ALASKA, AND I'M STRESSED. Mum and I are both off our brains with the challenge of packing for international travel, and wondering how our still-disrupted digestive systems are going to cope with the adventure.

Killarney is not well, but what can I do? I take her to the boarding kennel and say tender farewells, dreading that I may never see her again. I deliver a bundle of home-cooked food and a medicine kit to the kennel manager.

"Don't worry," she says. "I'll take good care of her."

The trip is heavy going, especially the long-haul flight across the Pacific. Alaska is every bit as beautiful as I expected, and it turns out I love cruising. I don't play bingo. I read books or nap. And I get to visit spectacular locations without having to pack-unpack each day. My hotel follows me around like a very big, very well groomed dog. I'm only seasick for a few hours when we hit rough water, but then we're back on the glassy surface of the Inside Passage again.

Other passengers have booked shore excursions

in every port, but I prefer to potter around these exotic towns and talk to locals about a life so very different to my own. The one exception is that I have to see sled dogs, and I don't care how touristy it is. There are options for flying to a glacier to cry "Mush!" but we take the closer-to-home alternative: a sled dog camp just outside Juneau, where in summer the sleds run on wheels.

Two of my senses are assailed: hearing, because the dogs are barking their heads off in excitement as they are hooked up to their harnesses, raring to get to work; sight, because they don't look anything like I'd expected. The sled dogs of my imagination are huge fluffy white dogs. These dogs are smaller and leaner and the colours of the rainbow. They are short-haired athletes, and their tails are wagging like mad. An Iditarod veteran shows us the gear they use to keep the dogs safe in wild weather.

Mum and I somehow score the front seat of the big wheeled sled. A man hands us disposable plastic ponchos to protect our clothes from the mud. It's a good thing, because there's plenty of Alaska thrown at us by the pounding feet of the dogs as they hurl us around corners and along a bumpy roadway. The dogs fly through the trees, joy in synchronised motion. I can't stop grinning.

Afterwards, I ask if it would be okay to pat the dogs, and am directed to the most sociable among the crew. A dog the colour of burnt cinnamon gazes at me out of melting brown eyes and leans against my leg as I rub her floppy ears. She feels like velvet and my heart is full.

❦

I TRY TO GET AN UPDATE FROM THE BOARDING KENNEL via email from various internet cafes, but have no success. After three weeks away I go to collect Killarney, wondering what I will find. There is a sign on the door: the kennel has been sold. The woman I know isn't there. I am given a dog so weak she can barely raise her head to look at me. I pick her up in my arms and cradle her against my chest. She weighs about as much as a butterfly.

As soon as I can get an appointment, I take her to Tom. His eyes tell me all I need to know.

"Take her home and feed her as often as you can. Just tiny amounts. See if she picks up at all. Give us a call and let us know."

It's a long, long week. I cover her in love. I pray for her. I cuddle her often, for both our sakes. I cook more painstakingly prepared lamb and try to tempt her with it. She nibbles at it, and sleeps a lot.

I take her back to the vet and she is slightly brighter and a few grams heavier. He nods. "Good. Keep going."

Maybe this is not the end. Not yet.

It's a long, slow, uphill fight, but she gradually becomes herself again. Weeks later, she's still in the bantamweight class, but she's once again waggling with the same enthusiasm she has had all her life. And that means I'm smiling too.

The global financial crisis is biting hard, and a few weeks before Christmas I'm chosen to join the latest round of retrenchments at my company. It hurts, but it's also wonderful, because I've known for a while that it's time to move on.

When I'm due to go camping for a week at Christmas, a holiday booked months ago, there's no way Killarney is going to a boarding kennel. I almost decide not to go away at all, but the vet tells me about a petsitter who left cards at their office just the day before.

I arrange to meet her. Her name is Angela, and it's a perfect name, because she's an angel with Killarney. She treats her with love and affection, and is highly intelligent. She reads all my endless instructions and understands their import.

"Don't worry, I'll take good care of her," says Angela.

This time when I return, I can see it's true.

BABY VESTS, THE LATEST IN CANINE COUTURE.

LESSON 15:
Joy is being yourself, not someone else

I HANDLE UNEMPLOYMENT DIFFERENT WAYS ON different days. One day I mope around reading Jane Austen and watching television. The next, I play loud music, attack all the junk that's built up in my house since Dad died, and write job applications. Most of the world is on summer break, so there's no urgency. Most of the business world is in crisis, so new positions in my field are rare.

Lauren is scouting for a change of job too, so we watch for interesting opportunities for each other. I tell her I've been called for an interview, and show her an ad for a job that might interest her.

"Looks a bit full-on for me," she says.

"Oh, most job ads make it sound like they need someone who could run an aircraft carrier in a warzone, but when you get there everyone seems to be eating cake and checking Facebook."

As I lick the wounds of the past few years, I think about how my ideal job ad would actually read:

Looking for someone who wants a gentle, easy life and plenty of time to take her dog to the vet.

But I know this too will pass.

I'm very deliberately looking for a part-time role. After four years in the corporate world I want to get back to the publishing work I really love to do.

I'm still writing job applications as new freelance clients start to come in. Before my redundancy package is all spent, the income is picking up. I'm starting to think I might freelance full-time, and stop applying for jobs. I'm much more connected than I was when I last tried setting up a new business twelve years earlier, new in town after seven years in Sydney.

No one can spell Write Angles, my business name that seemed clever in 1998, so I decide to change it. Every other name I can think of is already taken. I notice a business named after a racehorse and think: What if I name it after my dog? No one can spell Killarney, of course, so I finally settle on Small Blue Dog.

I set up a brand new website, and nervously write my first blog post. As a journalist and then an author, I'm used to being edited. I feel insecure that there's no one checking these scratchings before they go out into the world. Pressing the "publish" button all on my own is intimidating.

I join Twitter because everyone says it's essential for business these days. I say awkward, stilted things, trying to find my feet in 140 characters.

It's a whole new world.

❧

KILLARNEY IS GAINING WEIGHT ONE GRAM AT A TIME. I discover a butcher selling minced venison. It's naturally lean and I don't even have to cut it up. It sounds like appalling luxury to feed a dog venison, as though she's sitting down on satin cushions to a royal feast – but it's actually half the price of lamb. And the time saving for me is immense. Killarney loves it, and her digestion starts to stabilise.

"Add some bulk, but don't give her rice or wheat," says Tom.

"What about millet?"

"Sure. Give it a try."

I'm thinking of the delicious millet and pumpkin porridge I sometimes had for breakfast in Russia. Millet turns out to be hard to buy in Brisbane, but I'm determined, and I track it down. I cook it for two hours to ensure it's well softened. I'm possibly not the most focused chef in the world, but the smoke alarm lets me know when it's ready, and Killarney seems to quite enjoy the running-screaming that attends the process as well as the extra colour and texture in her bowl.

She also loves that I'm working from home most days. Now twelve years old, she spends much of the day snoozing beside my desk, doing a nice nose whistle when she's not snoring like a chainsaw. If I need to do a Skype meeting with a client, I put the dog outside so they don't think I've hired a personal barista.

Ever the exciting dog, she presents me with a new challenge.

She can no longer tolerate any of the regular flea control measures so necessary in Brisbane humidity, and they've got away from me. Fleabites on top of her grass allergies give us a 24/7 itchy and scratchy show. I experiment with tea tree oil. I wash her bedding in the hottest possible water every week. I flea-comb her daily. I buy a steam mop. I vacuum every day and steam mop every three days. I am in full-time servitude to fleas, and my floors have never been so clean. When unscheduled visitors arrive at my front door I no longer have to consider pretending I'm not home.

Allergy injections give Killarney a ferocious

hunger. When I find her chowing down on a plastic clothes peg, I realise I'll need to do a tour of the house to see what hungry-dog hazards might be at her eye level.

Her hair is thinning from a combination of scratching and aging and if I don't take action she's going to look like a Chinese crested – bald all over with a few tufts on her head. She smells strange due to the condition of her skin, and is fast becoming a dog that only a mother could love. And I do love her. When I look at her I don't see a wrinkly chin and bald patches. I see a courageous, optimistic, devoted friend who has faced challenge after challenge and still has plenty of waggle in her tail. I think back to a few years earlier when I watched a friend's elderly dog stagger round the house with half a coat of fur, and wondered what was wrong with it. They said, "He's fine. He's just old." Back then, I worried, but now, I believe them. I'm beginning to understand that the older a dog gets, it's only those closest who can truly evaluate the animal's quality of life. They can look a mess and still be happy.

I need to get garments for Killarney not as any kind of fashion statement, but to protect her skin from her own chewing, as well as to keep her warm when winter arrives and her natural coat is so thin.

Belinda Pollard | ⋯ | 221

"I think she might be allergic to synthetic fabrics," says Tom.

Oh great. Guess how many of the available dog garments are made from synthetics? If you guessed 100%, you'd be about right.

I haul out my sewing machine and create a warm jacket for her out of cotton flannelette unearthed from my fabric box, with old towels sandwiched between the layers. I quilt it to try to hold the whole lot together. It's so stiff it seems to move in a different direction than the dog when she corners too fast, but she's glad of it on cold winter nights, and it gradually softens with much washing.

I have the inspiration that a baby singlet (100% cotton baby vest) might just fit my Puddly. Fancy colours are $3 each, but baby blue and baby pink are only $2. I buy her one of each.

I begin to haunt the baby aisles at my local budget department store – something I always expected to do for my own children, but never did because of how life worked out. Now I'm doing it for a dog.

There are long-sleeved spencers – I cut the sleeves off at her elbow level – and little cotton sweaters with mysterious embroidered logos. I put them on her back-to-front, because her head sits back on her neck, not forward. One of them sags after a few hot washes and she keeps tripping on it, so I add elastic across the back to pull it up snug against her stomach. Gathers flare out over the base of her tail like a peplum, the latest in budget natural-fibre dog couture.

Killarney's mind seems to be going the way of her hair. One evening she's sitting contentedly at my feet while I watch television. I've just given her a tummy rub with my foot through all the layers of cotton she's wearing. Suddenly she leaps up and goes trotting around the house.

Click-click-click go her claws on the tiles. Then into another room. And another. It dawns on me that she's looking for me.

"Killarney!" She stops in mid-search and looks in my direction, then runs towards me in delight. She does a happy dance in front of me.

I've seen Alzheimer's in humans, so I wonder what might lie ahead. But she doesn't seem to get much worse, just a little (more) eccentric.

I trade stories with Lauren, because Cocoa has hit the dementia years as well. He is now running a slalom course up and down her polished-wood hallway all day. She endures it well, but her husband finds it a little tiring if the cat does it all night.

Killarney's hearing is going, too. If she starts

barking I have to shout quite loudly in order for her to hear me telling her to be quiet. I'm sure the neighbours enjoy this.

But then she's lying in her basket when a raging storm comes over one evening. I wait for her to get up and do the storm dance as thunder rumbles around us, but she just lies there comfortably. Aging is not all bad.

❧

IN MY CLEANING UP, I STUMBLE UPON MY JOURNALISM photo ID from when I was twenty. I can't believe how bright-eyed and clear-skinned I was. And I remember how much energy and joy I wasted comparing myself to the airbrushed magazine girls instead of just celebrating how God had made me.

It strikes me that when I'm in my sixties, I'll look back at photos of me now and think: What was I worrying about?

I make a stand that day, plant a flag. In future when I'm thinking about feeling insecure again I'll say to myself: What rubbish, Belinda. You look fine. You look great. You look like you.

❧

I DECIDE TO TAKE ANOTHER SHOT AT MY NOVEL, AND DIG out all my research, and the 11,000 words that have been lying fallow for five years. I still don't know if I can build and sustain a world for 90,000 words, but I decide it's time to find out. I discover some competitions for manuscript development, where the winner receives guidance while completing their book, along with the opportunity to put it in front of one of the Big Six publishers. Crucial to the plan, it gives me a deadline, something I have always found motivating.

I write some more words, and then nervously send off my manuscript. No one else has ever read this book. Is it any good or not?

The results appear on the website. I'm not on the shortlist. I feel miserable, and lose traction.

A couple of months later I try again, with no success. I pick myself up, write some more, and apply a third time. By now, the manuscript has hit 30,000 words. I head to the website the day the shortlist is announced.

I scan down the list.

"Belinda Pollard, Poison Bay."

I stop, and breathe, and look again. Have I misread it? No, I haven't. My name really is there.

I'm walking on air all day. I can't believe it. I

can't concentrate on my work. I can't remember the last time I was so excited.

I go on to win a fellowship. The day I get the news, I book flights to Sydney for the writing retreat that's part of my prize. My mind buzzes with silly, mundane details about what I'll take with me and how I'll catch the train up to the mountains. But even the joy of winning can't compete with the sensation of making the shortlist, and I puzzle about why that would be. Finally, it dawns on me that the shortlist was the turning point. It was the first time I'd had the slightest indication that someone might think my novel was worth reading. The shortlist made me think my dream might come true after all.

❧

I'M ASKED TO WRITE A SERIES OF BIBLE MEDITATIONS ON "trauma" for my UK publisher, and it's apt. The year begins with my own city of Brisbane consumed by floodwaters, and a fearful night for me as I evacuate with a few valuables and my dog and wonder if there'll be anything to go back to. My house survives, but bridges will take years to rebuild, the city's "food bowl" is under a layer of mud and in a city of two million it's hard even to find bread. Then, Cyclone Yasi hits north Queensland – five hundred kilometres wide and as strong as Hurricane Katrina. Primary industries are devastated, and the bananas I eat to calm my stomach when I'm stressed cost anything up to fourteen times their usual price.

An earthquake crushes Christchurch, New Zealand, and I weep as I watch the rescue efforts on television, but it's so hard to look away. It has also flattened a beautiful coastal town I'd wandered through and grown attached to during a visit just weeks before. I wear the handmade cotton pyjamas I bought there and wonder if that sweet little local business will have any future now.

A tsunami sweeps away thousands of souls in Japan and one of my charity clients needs me to chase personal reports for their newsletter, so I'm bouncing emails around a disaster zone for days.

There's a part in the Bible that talks about creation "groaning", and I groan along with it, wishing life on this planet didn't have to be so hard. One of the heaviest blows however is not global but personal. A dear friend whose support kept me going through some gloomy times dies of the cancer we thought she was beating. If only I'd managed to catch up with her at Christmas like we'd planned.

Even though it's tough, I can sense I'm dealing with these traumas much better than I would have a couple of years ago. I'm more content, more resilient, more determined to bounce back.

❦

THE CREAKING OF KILLARNEY'S BASKET WAKES ME AT 4.30 am. As it happens, I've only been asleep an hour, after tossing and turning half the night. I take her out to the Pet Loo for a wee, and then back to bed. But she can't settle. She doesn't seem to know where she is. And then she starts whimpering.

I walk around and around with her, in my pjs, getting chilled to my bone marrow. Is she in pain, or just confused? I can hardly detect her heartbeat, and when I can, it seems faint and erratic. Heavens above, is she having a heart attack and mistaking the pain for toilet pains?

Could this be "it", even though she's been so well? Strangely, I'm not panicking or distressed. I know I'll miss her like arms or legs once she's gone, but she is thirteen years old, and I've finally accepted that she is only mine on loan, not to keep. If the worst does actually happen, I want to know that I took the trouble to make her comfortable and unafraid. I know those are the memories that bring comfort later.

I pick up the confused little wanderer in a big

hug, and loll across an armchair with her in my arms, trying to find a position in which we can both go to sleep. In my arms she knows where she is, and she quietens. I can hardly breathe with her weight on my chest. My back will scream at me tomorrow. She tries to curl up on my belly with my arm as a pillow, but her head keeps falling sideways.

Half an hour later she is still with us, so I make an executive decision to put her back in her basket. Near-death experiences do have time limitations. I lie on the lounge with a hastily-grabbed blanket over me, one hand on the dog. Every time she tries to get up and walk around again, I quiet her with my hand. Eventually she settles and goes off to sleep.

At 6.30 am my alarm goes off. Killarney opens one eye to peer sleepily at me as I shuffle tiredly around the house. She is very warm and snug, thank you.

Three hours later Killarney is out in the palace, basking in the morning sun in her basket after enjoying a delicious venison breakfast. There are no lingering signs of her distress in the early hours, and she doesn't really know why I'm looking quite so haggard.

ero

THE FELLOWSHIP I'VE WON FOR MY MANUSCRIPT MEANS a week's writing retreat at Katoomba in the Blue Mountains. Mum volunteers to look after the dog for me, but with Killarney's dementia and deteriorating eyesight she needs to stay in her familiar environment. That means she will get twice-daily visits for food and cuddles, and be sleeping out in her kennel at nights, within her snake-proof palace.

I worry that she'll be miserable without me, since the weather has been so cold, and she is so old.

"Why don't you get her used to the kennel now," Mum says. "You should sleep her in it anyway. The noises she makes in that basket are always waking you up. And *she'll* probably sleep better too."

Killarney may have started life as an outdoor dog, but she's been an indoor dog for years now. You can't just snap your fingers and change a thing like that.

And besides, I like knowing she is near.

But the trip away is approaching, and something must be done. I decide to trial sleeping her in her kennel for one night, to see how it goes. It will be hard for both of us to make this leap, but it's better done now while I'm here to sort out any problems and hopefully come up with solutions.

I decide to keep the palace light on all night, so

she can find her way if she needs a toilet trip. I make a flap for the kennel's arched doorway out of canvas, to keep the warm in and the light out. I make a nest of towels and flannelette inside the kennel, piled up in a huge arc around the sides and back of the kennel, so that she will be lying on soft and warm, and enfolded in soft and warm.

At bedtime, I put on her heavy winter jacket that I sewed for her myself, and take her outside.

"In you get!" say I, putting on my positive voice. I can't let her see how horrified I am. She looks momentarily puzzled, but then hops in happily enough. I settle her, pat her, croon to her just a little even though she probably can't hear it. She snuggles down into the big pile of flannelette, and wriggles her chin into a nice comfy position, supported by softness. I let the door flap drop, and then I go inside and close the door, trying to walk in a light-hearted and confidence-inspiring manner, like it's the most natural thing in the world I could do.

I go to my own bed and lie there bereft, no basket creaking with restless dog in the bedroom doorway. My dreams are weird whenever I sleep, but mostly I'm awake. I've left my window wide open, so I can easily hear any Killarney-noises in the night. Is she getting up for the loo, only to wander and bump into things and forget where her bed is, falling at last into exhausted sleep on the cold, hard concrete, confused and unloved?

I am alert and ready to rescue. I hear nothing.

Is she dead?

In the morning I go straight to the back door. I cannot see a dog anywhere through the glass and I steel myself. "Be sensible Belinda. You can cope. Of course she's not dead. If she's got herself caught behind anything in the night, we can sort it out."

As the sliding door groans in its tracks, the kennel door flap twitches, and Killarney emerges sleepily from her cocoon, stretching luxuriously, fresh and rested, tail all a-wag.

She loves it out there.

ᔕᔭ

I WRITE FOUR THOUSAND WORDS A DAY ON MY NOVEL while I'm at Katoomba. I walk the mountains in icy winds and imagine things. The historic house has five bedrooms for writers, each with a writing room attached. It is sheer luxury to write fiction all day for a whole week, and discuss the ups and downs with other writers at night.

My manuscript consultant puts me through my paces, challenging my characters and why they've decided to go on such a crazy trek in the wilderness. I'd say yes to such an invitation myself, so it hasn't occurred to me that my characters probably wouldn't.

"What's your theme?" she says. "What's the book really about?"

"Um…" I didn't even know that mystery/thriller novels, the kind sold in airport bookstores, were supposed to have a "metanarrative", so new am I at this. "I think it might be greed."

Staying in a house full of writers has its moments. The staff go home at night, leaving us to our own devices. The previous group were convinced there was a ghost, and one of my group declares there has been moaning in the wall behind his head overnight. "Do you mean the wind in the chimney?" say I.

I'm less prosaic on the last night, when there are only two of us left in the big old creaking house. We keep bumping into each other in the hallway in the small hours, both hearing noises. My concern is about human visitors, however. Writers can be a vague lot. We'd just discovered there was a key in the outside of one of the doors most of the week.

Back home, I find Killarney has managed just fine without me.

I make the bold decision to continue the outdoor

sleeping. I can see how much better she sleeps out there in her cocoon, hardly stirring all night, so I've decided to be a grown-up about it. It's the right thing to do. And now that I have overcome the separation anxiety, I'm sleeping better too, without the continual creaking of the basket.

ᎯᎬ

I FINISH *POISON BAY* BECAUSE I'VE GOT A DEADLINE. Somehow, it comes out of my fingers onto the keyboard, even though I wasn't sure if it would. I discover that it's not about greed, but forgiveness, and what can happen when it is withheld and turns sour. I send it to my manuscript consultant and another beta reader. I rework it in response to their feedback, then send it off to Random House, nervously wondering. I wait, and try not to fantasise about six-figure book advances.

I wait some more. Surely I'd have heard by now, if they wanted it? But they're busy, so maybe not. Eventually, I receive a feedback report, and it has some positive things to say as well as intriguing suggestions. I read it several times just to be sure there's no offer included.

I'm disappointed, and I lose traction for a while, but I'm not destroyed. There are so many options now. Publishing worldwide is undergoing a Copernican revolution. Most of the major publishers in Australia are newly open to unsolicited manuscripts. I have the email address of the CEO of one major publisher, given at a writer's conference a couple of years before. And Random House indicate they'd be happy to see it again when I've done my next rewrite.

I'm not afraid of hard work. I feel sure that my book will exist in the world one day. The adventure will be in finding out how.

For the moment though, it is enough that I have written it, after longing to do so for so much of my life. I have written a novel.

NOTHING BEATS A NICE NAP.
(EXCEPT MAYBE A CUDDLE.)

LESSON 16:
Be content, and joy might surprise you

ANOTHER WINTER IS DRAWING TO AN END. THE SUN IS warm and bright today, after a deluge on the weekend. Killarney is curled in her basket near my desk, doing her contented-bumblebee snore. It's much less disruptive to my concentration than the motocross snore she was doing yesterday. Today's baby vest is pink.

After months of carefully choreographed over-feeding from which she digests maybe only fifty percent, she is pleasantly solid again. Enough weight to give her some reserves if she gets sick, without being so heavy that it makes the arthritis worse. And her winter coat has filled out all the patches from the Summer of Fleas, giving her a fluffy and lush look. It's hard to believe this dog could have been at death's door eighteen months ago.

She might occasionally lose her grip on the ground, especially when cornering too fast, but she still has the enthusiasm to corner too fast, and she's up on her feet again promptly, heading for the next adventure.

And she is sleeping deeply and well, thanks to me finally letting her return to the kennel that makes her feel snug and safe.

This is a well dog. Old, but well.

ↂ

IT IS ANNUAL-VACCINATION DAY FOR KILLARNEY, AND she is delirious about going in the car as usual. She knows the signs. If I pick up my handbag and then close the back door with her inside it, it means she is going too. Oh happy day! Leap and squeal and bark.

She's hardly been anywhere lately, except to the vet. And yet she loves to go in the car. Go figure.

Her squeals turn to whines as we get close to the vet's office. She knows how many twists and turns there are between home and there. Exactly how many twists and turns and which way they tilt. She loves Tom and Hayley, but not their thermometers or scalpels.

As we approach along the footpath, I can see through the glass door that the vet's waiting room contains a woman with a small fluffy pup on her lap. Thankfully, Killarney hasn't seen the fluffy pup, due to the reflections on the glass and her aged eyesight.

I slide the door open a crack and ask the woman what time her appointment is. It's before mine, so I say, "I'll wait out here until you go in. If I bring my dog in she'll want to play with yours." "Play" is code for "leap upon, growling", but I see no reason to be specific.

We parade up and down the footpath outside the vet's surgery as traffic rumbles past a few feet away. Killarney is high-stepping, her head erect, her tail banner waving. It may just be that she thinks she's escaped going to the vet, but I can't get over how young and vital she looks.

Once inside on the big metal table, Killarney sits close to me, and gazes fixedly at Tom with huge, unblinking eyes. He swoops down from his great height and returns the eye contact from a few inches away but she continues to stare, agog. He laughs and gives her a pat.

We commence with the dreaded thermometer and after a quick attempt to climb over me and out of here, I get Killarney to settle and put up with it. She doesn't break the thermometer this year like she did last year when she sent it flying across the room to release little globules of mercury all over the floor. Her temperature is perfect.

Next he listens to her heart and lungs, for quite a long time, and asks me how old she is.

"Fourteen."

"Really?" He shakes his head in amazement. "She's doing well."

Hayley has had to pop out to the waiting room for a moment and Tom is already swabbing between Killarney's shoulder blades. He seems to be assuming I can hold her still enough. I am paranoid because last year there was wriggling, shrieking (mostly from Killarney), and a bent needle. I have learned that old dogs lose their subcutaneous fat, and it makes injections tricky. But this time all is done in a moment without so much as a whimper.

I need to ask Tom a few things before we leave. Killarney has swivelled to face the exit door, her back turned unequivocally toward him. She is pressed up against me, her shoulder almost disappearing into my belly. I ask Tom, "Could she get any further away from you, do you think?"

He laughs. "She'd have to be on the other side of you."

"Well, she did try that earlier."

He says, "With very young and old dogs, we

recommend bringing forward their vaccination so they've developed full immunity before the hot weather starts."

"I'll do that next year then." I glance down at my aged sweetie and her eyelashes that have turned white at the roots, and add an afterthought. "If I've still got her then, that is."

His answer is confident. "Oh, you'll still have her."

I hope he's right. And maybe the year after that.

On Twitter I saw an R.I.P. for a much-loved fourteen year old dog. "We will miss you for a long, long time," was that dog mother's farewell message. I know that day is coming for me too, sooner or later. People say, "You just want it to be later." No, actually. I want it to be never.

But unless something unexpected happens to me first, I'm going to be bereft eventually. This week, this year, three year's time – who knows? But there'll be plenty of time for crying then.

I know I can't have her forever, but for now, I do. I love this little scrap, and I thank God for bringing her into my life. The companionship, the laughter, the drama, the heartache, the responsibility – all of it. Even the inconvenience of having to go home at night to take care of her I've learned to recognise as a blessing; never underestimate the benefit of being needed. Who knows how much longer she has, or where her journey might take us both? Her health might decline, her cancer could return, her dementia might accelerate, things could get a bit crazy. I'll be there for her just as she has been there for me.

But I've learned that there's no joy living in the shadow of an uncertain future. Her persistent optimism in the face of so many disasters has challenged me to look at life differently – to complain less and rejoice more. I've decided to live in the warmth of the present with a happy little dog snoozing in the spring sunshine, and words to write on my screen.

My goal now is not to prolong her life by a few scant weeks by hunting out health problems and stamping them out aggressively. While ever she is happy, enjoying her meals and her cuddles, I'm not going to think about problems. When bleaker times come we'll cope. If I'd taken this attitude years ago, we might all have had a more relaxing time of it. But I hadn't learned it then.

Now is the time to celebrate this crazy never-say-die hound and enjoy every minute we get to spend together. To laugh at her acrobatics. Giggle at her loud delight when she realises we're playing hide-and-seek. Be gentle with her failings because she can't remember what she was meant to do, or where she was meant to do it. Cuddle her and touch her for both our sakes, even just a tickle with a foot on my way past to some other part of the house. Let her sniff the garden beds despite their hazards so she can revel in her one remaining full-strength sense, while I watch like a hawk for anything slithery-deadly that might be concealed among the leaves.

To stop worrying so much that it spoils the adventure. To enjoy now, because really that is the only time that any of us can be sure of, no matter how many plans we make or how powerful we stupidly think we are.

For as long as I have Killarney and then when she is gone, I will grab life by the scruff of the neck and shake every last drop of joy out of it. And wrestle it, if I have to.

Afterword

IF YOU CAN BELIEVE IT, KILLARNEY ALMOST MADE IT to seventeen – nearly one hundred and twenty in dog years. Where cancer, snakes and big dogs had failed, extreme old age had the last, softly-spoken word. I would have added the final stages of her journey to this book, but somehow it didn't feel right. That's because soon after I wrote the ending you've just read, we became a two-dog family and life changed shape again.

Rufus is the red cattle dog mix you'll often see on my Facebook page or Instagram feed. He'd already been with us two years before the time came to grieve Killarney, and although I didn't think anything could help dry my tears, he did indeed become my "red healer". A shy and studious type, he is the opposite of Killarney in almost every way. They do, however, have in common two abilities: to create chaos and to make me laugh out loud.

Killarney + Rufus = a whole new season of growth for Belinda. But that's a story for another book. (Stay tuned.)

This book had to be Killarney's and hers alone.

Thank you, God of all creatures, for giving me this sweet little friend. I still have a lot to learn, but I am a more determined, kinder, more joyful person for having known her.

From the Author

THANK YOU FOR SHARING A LITTLE PIECE OF MY HEART. It has been quite a journey delving into past challenges to write this book, and yet it has also brought the joyful moments alive again. If any of this encourages you in your life, then it has all been worth it.

I don't have the marketing budget of the big publishers, so if you'd like to support me the most wonderful thing you can do is tell others about this book. Write an honest review, tell your friends, alert a book club, tell a librarian, give a copy as a gift.

That novel I was writing? I finished it, and it's out now, too! *Poison Bay* is even available in Large Print. You'll find the details on the following pages.

Thank you so much for being part of my writing, and may your life be blessed.

Belinda Pollard is an award-winning mystery author and former journalist who used to chuckle about people who treated their pets like children – until it happened to her. Her hobbies now include dog-walking in the rain and watching dog-training videos. She is a speaker, publishing consultant and book editor. She lives in Australia, travels the world (when she can find a good petsitter), and blogs at belindapollard.com.

Also by Belinda Pollard

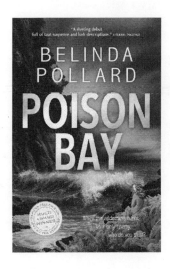

Poison Bay

ISBN: 978-0-9942098-0-1

Large Print: 978-0-6482672-3-2

Winner: Varuna Fellowship, IPPY Silver Medal

When the wilderness is not your only enemy, who do you trust?

Television reporter Callie Brown likes big cities and good coffee. But, running from a broken heart, she agrees to join old friends at the strangest of reunions: a trek into New Zealand's most savage and remote mountains. What she doesn't know is that someone wants them all dead...

"Taut suspense and lush descriptions." Literary Inklings

"Satisfyingly insightful." Margaret Newman

"By turns shocking, satisfying, tragic, and poignant, but ultimately life-affirming." Debbie Young's Reading Life

"So far this is my favourite fiction read of the

year." Clare O'Beara, Amazon UK Top 500
Reviewer

Also vailable in German:
Verschollen in der Poison Bay
ISBN: 978-0-9942098-7-0

Made in the USA
Coppell, TX
19 August 2020